"I'm Adult! Aren't I!"

First published in 2008 by

Rubin Mass Ltd
POB 990, Jerusalem 91009, Israel
rmass@barak.net.il

www.imadultarenti.com
orders@imadultarenti.com

British Library Cataloguing in Publication Data
A catalogue record for this book is available from the British Library.

Printed by Lightning Source

ISBN
hbk 978-965-09-0225-4
pbk 978-965-09-0266-7

Project management by Sean Kingston Publishing Services
www.seankingston.co.uk

"I'M ADULT! AREN'T I!"

*

Understanding Juvenile Delinquency
and
Creating Adults out of Children

*

THE CASE FOR
A FORMAL
RITE OF PASSAGE

Geoffrey Ben-Nathan

RUBIN MASS
JERUSALEM

CONTENTS

Part V The Japanese Way

Part VI The Power of Ritual and Myth

Part VII Rite-of-Passage Experience

Part VIII Passage-time: Proposal for a Present-Day Rite of Passage

For my wife Margaret

and

Russ and the graffiti warriors

PREFACE

The words of this book's title, "I'm Adult! Aren't I!", were the response given by an anonymous adolescent when I asked him why he was smoking. This was way back in 1976 at a chance encounter at a London Probation office.

"I'm Adult! Aren't I!" presents its readers with what I believe is an entirely new perspective on the root cause of most juvenile delinquency and adolescent anti-social behaviour: western society has failed to realise that children need to be matured into adults in a very formal way. If left to chance, results can be, and frequently are, disastrous. What is now urgently needed therefore is a state-supervised programme of socialisation, a state-supervised rite of passage. After decades of no-progress, this is now the only way ahead.

The book argues that anti-social behaviour and juvenile delinquency are children's own impromptu substitutes for rite of passage. They are the ad hoc 'programme' that many children initiate for themselves, in the absence of anything official. Children, these days, seem to be in a headlong rush to gain what they believe to be adult status. This book claims that the objective of ad hoc anti-social behaviour is the attempt, usually unsuccessful, to discard childhood status. If children are going to be successful in their desire, they are going to need formal state help.

"I'm Adult! Aren't I!" asserts that the socialisation of children into young adults is a process equivalent in importance to education itself. Just as there is a Ministry of Education, so there may need to be, ungainly as it sounds, a Ministry of Socialisation. The measures suggested in the book for a contemporary rite of passage for our own society no doubt require such an initiative if they are to be implemented – as would, I believe, almost any other suggestion for a viable rite of passage.

In making the case, readers are introduced to the way socialisation of youths proceeds in highly ritualised societies. Two such societies, the Maasai and the Japanese, are explored in detail. Both mature their youth very successfully; but they do so in very different ways. They are a reservoir of ideas.

This leads to deeper consideration of ritual and rite of passage; ritual's astonishing power to transform human beings from one status to another; but is, we ask, Western society too sophisticated to embrace ritual and the rite-of-passage phenomenon?

We note the existence of apparently parallel modes of behaviour in the youth of Western and highly ritualised societies: the prevalence of what may be called 'angry young man' syndrome; and how the capricious force we label 'Destiny' seems to be propitiated by youth everywhere. Initiation rituals such as scarification or circumcision without anaesthetic take their toll of injury and death among the youth in some, but not all, highly ritualised societies; whilst in Western society, youth court danger by playing games of 'chicken' – of which drug-taking, joy-riding and the latest fad of tomb-stoning are but a few of many. Even the more positive approach of taking a gap year to travel the world can end up with Destiny's intervention by way of road accident or misadventure.

We examine a fascinating experiment to introduce rite of passage to modern American youngsters. In the final part of the book, we unveil proposals for a contemporary and international rite-of-passage programme for children in Western society. Life-skills, life-experiences and voluntary service at home and abroad make up its content. This programme is always informed by principles derived from the investigation of traditional and highly ritualised societies.

If this book has its ultimate influence, it will be instrumental in redirecting the course by which children in Western society are raised and transformed into adults. In the first instance though, it may be judged a success if it does no more than convince the Establishment that the real source of our current woes with young people derives from the absence of formal rite of passage. For too long we have talked about the causes of crime without knowing what they really are; worse, for too long innocent young lives have been blighted, victims of forces of whose existence they are unaware and whose power they cannot control.

The book makes it abundantly clear that successful rite of passage cannot be introduced 'tomorrow morning'. Any rite-of-passage proposal, including the one put forward in this book, requires changes to law. In making the necessary proposals, one hears a chorus of 'you *can't* do this, you'll *never* get that through'. Theory is one thing, practice quite another. If rite of passage is traumatising for young people, it may be even more so for the society that attempts to put it into practice! This is a problem one just has to face. As they say: 'No pain, no gain'.

Having said all this, I know in my bones that formal transition, rite of passage, is the right, indeed, as I have said, the *only* way to proceed. It alone offers the necessary transformation: and so, for many youngsters this will be a transformation from despair to hope; from overgrown child to confident young adult; from incarcerated young offender to valued young citizen; from liability to asset; and, trite as it may sound, from zero to hero.

Geoffrey Ben-Nathan
Jerusalem, June 2008

FOREWORD

'IM *ADOL*' ANAI?'

There were just the two of us. I was in my mid-thirties; he was 15, if that. We were waiting – for differing reasons, I imagine – for the local probation officer to return from lunch. It was a hot summer afternoon in 1976. There was nothing to do but to chat or ignore each other, so I embarked on idle small-talk. After a minute or two, I focused on his cigarette which, clearly, I was meant to. He brandished it between his thin bony fingers, controlling it with considerable dexterity.

'So you're into smoking then,' I said, nonchalantly stating the obvious.

'Well, I'm *adol'* anai?'

'Sorry?' I couldn't make any sense of the garbled syllables.

'I'm *adol'* anai?'

Ah! Got it! 'I'm-adult-aren't-I.' That was what the boy was saying.

'Oh yes, of course,' I replied, meaning how stupid of me. I had repaired my momentary lapse. Once again, we were two adults killing time together.

Our man returned from lunch. The young boy went in. I waited my turn.

I pondered his words: 'I'm adol' anai?'

This poor pathetic little chap wasn't adult. He was anything but. And yet he sought to convey that he was. He was possessed of an overwhelming desire to 'grow up', or, if not to grow up, to put as much clear blue water as he could between childhood and his current adolescence.

I then had a moment of certainty. I was sure more than ever before of two things: first, antisocial behaviour, juvenile delinquency, call it what you will, is a status-transition problem; and secondly, as a status-transition problem, the solution to it would come from the field of anthropology where the question of status-transition has been most thoroughly investigated.

Rightly or wrongly, I felt I had a special role to play. Given time, I felt, I'd hopefully be able to make a special – perhaps even a decisive – contribution. Why?

A piece of background.

BACKGROUND

My father died in May 1962 when I was 17. I had left school early at the age of 16 to look after his business. There was no smooth passage from school to university. My would-be university years, from 18 to 21, were spent in Islington running an electrical shop. It was hard but enjoyable.

Circumstances changed. At 22, a university career became possible. I entered London University's School of Oriental and African Studies to read for an Honours Degree in African Studies. The degree comprised three elements: Anthropology (the study of 'other' cultures); the study of a language spoken in Africa (I chose Amharic, the principal language of Ethiopia); and Linguistics, the social science that investigates the sounds, grammar and syntax of language the world over.

The course was phenomenal. My teachers were almost all published world authorities. I felt privileged. I *was* privileged. I still feel privileged. It was a first-class arts education.

There was only one problem – me! I spent my time at university enjoying myself. There were parties and politics. I got myself elected as vice-president of the students' union; I spent the last two years of the course courting. Somehow or other, you know how it is, study was always put off. How could I complain when I emerged in 1968 with a rather poor third-class degree.

Shortly after we married in 1970, a couple of years after my university studies had concluded, my wife Margaret came home with a book from our local W.H. Smiths. It was a hardback that had been remaindered – not a promising endorsement. I don't know why she thought I'd like it; maybe it was the design on its dust cover: a hat stand, an umbrella *in* the hat stand, civil servant's bowler *on* it – and a spear *next* to it.

THE COMPANY SAVAGE

I was immediately put off by the title, *The Company Savage – Life in the Corporate Jungle*. I didn't like the word 'savage'. In a book whose theme is cultural equivalence, the word is unhelpful. To me, the use of the word 'savage' in the title undermined the very thesis that the book so successfully affirms – that so-called 'savages' are everything but. But I didn't write the book, Martin Page did; and no-one seems to have created a fuss. Quite the contrary, the title is very popular.

I read *The Company Savage* from cover to cover and found it a revelation. The book is, as stated, about cultural equivalence, and is a manual of business and social management technique. Boss, staff, wife, kids and mother-in-law problems, it tells us, assail Stock Exchange Man and Stone Age Man alike. It matters little if you live in New York or New Guinea. In both locations human beings require techniques for managing their problems. Page analyses these techniques and sometimes finds modern man copying his tribal counterpart without realising it. Furthermore, he suggests that often, when modern man is *not* following in the footsteps of his tribal counterpart, he ought to be doing so. Look hard, and you'll find great sophistication in highly ritualised societies. Indeed, having analysed their conduct, Page exposes the presence of tribal business and social syndromes so deeply embedded in our own culture that we don't recognise them: we often can't see the wood for the trees.

The book created a huge impression. Single-handedly, so-to-speak, it brought alive four long years of dry and academic university study. In doing so it opened my mind and gave relevance to what had hitherto been entirely scholastic and somewhat sterile. In the next section I discuss Page's book in more detail, given that its influence upon me – and upon the present book – has been formative.

The Company Savage is very funny and highly readable. Page claims to create a 'new' science which he calls Tribology. (This, by the way, makes *two* sciences of the same name.[1*]) Page's science is dedicated, he says, to showing that 'the jargon and the practices of our business world are synthetic imitations of tribal customs perfected by centuries of trial and error'.

To give you an idea, I quote from the book's dust-cover blurb (with each technique's definition explained after it as per the book's 'Glossary of Tribological Terms'):

Here in *The Company Savage,* the business executive will learn the meaning of:

- The Lugbur Curse (a technique probably devised by the elders of the Lugbur tribe of Uganda to suppress over-ambitious subordinates, now used in business),
- The Rajah' Trap (a device believed to be the invention of an Indian ruler who, by encouraging over-specialising in his immediate subordinates, removed and excluded potential challengers from positions from which they could make a plausible bid for

1 The original meaning of Tribology was 'the study of friction, wear, lubrication, and the design of bearings: the science of interacting surfaces in relative motion' (Oxford Concise Dictionary).

power. Now (1976) found in the electronics and other technologically advanced industries),

- The Mambwe Dodge (a technique of concealing one's true wealth from others, particularly one's nearest and dearest, by appearing to be constantly in debt),
- The Horomorun Paradox (the paradox that the more one earns, the smaller becomes that proportion of one's salary one is allowed to spend),
- The Yam Factor (1. Positive Function (YF-PF): A force which ensures that wives gain more benefit from their husband's incomes than their husbands do. 2. Negative Function (YF-NF): A force that creates a boomerang effect on people who seek to gain prestige by buying prestige symbols),
- The Uttar Pradesh Effect (the process by which profit-obsessed *Contract Teams* normally decline into bankruptcy).

If he is a shrewd operator he will be wise to study and digest:

- The Law of Executive Insolvency.

And finally he will come to look upon his Tax Inspector in an entirely new light.

All in all, Page deduces and defines over sixty business and social syndromes. For me, Page restored the *anthropos* (Greek for mankind) to anthropology. He makes anthropology universal – the study of 'all' of mankind. In my university course, I never felt that it had been. Tacitly, there had been 'them' and 'us'. Study of 'them' was anthropology; study of 'us' – man in 'developed' society – was separately defined. That was sociology.

Secondly, Page exploded another tacit assumption: that we have a lot to learn *about* highly ritualised societies but nothing to learn *from* them and that, on the contrary, they have everything to learn from us; insofar as we spend time learning about their cultures, it's mainly to enable us to smooth their path towards us.

Those words quoted above, 'tribal customs perfected by centuries of trial and error' are words which resonate with me. Such customs command respect. They demand investigation. What are they? Are there more?

IN PRAISE OF PAGE

The Company Savage, is unique. In this book, we learn there is much to learn *from* highly ritualised societies. Their ways and our ways are capable of being united. The book is a wonderful example of 'applied anthropology'. By comparing tribal and modern experiences, Page has provided powerful insight into some of the deepest motivations in human nature. So far as I know, the book is not, nor ever has been, on undergraduate reading lists, which is a great pity!

I was a businessman, and Page's book became my business bible. It still is. I contacted Page and we met on several occasions. I pronounced myself his devoted disciple only to find I was second in line. One Christopher Frank Kearton (d. 1992), Lord Kearton of Whitchurch, OBE, FRS, had got there first. Courtaulds, Hill Samuel and the British National Oil Corporation were prodigiously successful under his leadership. Can there be any doubt that all this success was founded upon Lord Kearton's knowledge and application of the principles of Tribology?

The obituary of Martin Page (1938–2003) appeared in *The Times* on 16 September 2003. He was eminently well qualified to write *The Company Savage,* having read anthropology at Cambridge. A distinguished journalist who turned author after failing eyesight cut short his newspaper career, he had been Chief Foreign Correspondent in the sixties for Beaverbrook Newspapers in three major locations – Paris, Moscow and Rome. He reported the insurgency in Algeria and the wars in the Congo and Vietnam.

His obituary tells us that *The Company Savage* was a best-seller in Germany and Japan. But this was just one of several books he wrote on many disparate themes. An extremely talented journalist, learned in many fields, Martin Page has been, as you must have gathered by now, a seminal influence on my life and thinking.

TIME FOR ANTHROPOLOGISTS TO GET THEIR HANDS DIRTY

I am not a professional anthropologist and have no career background, nor am I known in any part of the criminological establishment. Yet in this book I have attempted to present the causes of, and a proposed solution to, the problem of juvenile crime. Society craves an answer to this long-standing scourge. The curse of youth antisocial behaviour demands a remedy. Antisocial behaviour blights the life of the young and the culture within which it occurs. If the proper causes of the phenomenon can be identified, society won't care where the revelation comes from. Moreover, my studies, reading and private research in schools, colleges and young offender institutions have furnished me with a unique perspective.

The view that there is a direct cause and effect between failed status-transition and antisocial behaviour has not, so far as I know, been previously advanced. Nor, too, the idea that highly ritualised societies must be a first port of call for theoretical inspiration; nor, finally, the idea that only a formal rite of passage will help put an end to antisocial behavioural mayhem.

I am not alone in the view that anthropology could have contributed more than it has. Many comments to this effect have come from within the profession. In a UK anthropological journal, Cecil Helman, Professor of Medical Anthropology at Brunel University writes:

> Here [the UK] many anthropology departments have regarded 'applied anthropology' as a contradiction in terms, putting the emphasis more on observing than on participating. Applied anthropology was seen as not 'pure' scholarship but rather as contaminated by its close engagement with practical and policy issues. [...] In the years to come it will no longer be enough for most anthropologists to be merely academic voyeurs, analysing the situation from the sidelines. [...] My hope is that in the future different types of professional experience, even if they originate beyond the borders of anthropology, will be increasingly welcomed into the discipline, and encouraged to contribute even further to its development. Such an eclectic approach can only benefit and enrich, anthropology.
>
> 'Why Medical Anthropology Matters', *Anthropology Today*, Feb. 2006, pp. 3–4

I can't and don't claim professional experience. But it's good to read of this catholic attitude, which is a welcome call for contribution from all quarters.

MEANWHILE ...

It was about 8:30 am. The phone rang. I answered it. It was my friend Russ. We'd had lunch together a couple of days back.

'I hate to say this,' he said, 'but you're r ... r ... r ... right!'

'Thank you,' I replied. 'But, as a matter of interest, about what?'

'You remember the graffiti kids?'

I remembered the graffiti kids. Russ runs a market stall in an Essex town. At lunch, he told me all about the graffiti kids. They're aged around 12 to 15, decked out in designer gear and they parade around on bicycles. Kudos accrues to the most daredevil – whoever puts his 'tag' in the most dangerous spot. Russ said they were all scrupulously honest. Whenever he gave credit for soft drinks or whatever, they always paid back. It confirmed, he surmised, their perception of adult behaviour.

'What about the graffiti kids?'

'Well, when we had lunch, you challenged me to call one of them "a child". Well, I did. I found an excuse to start a sentence: Of course, as a child, you ... I never got beyond the "you".'

'What happened?'

'Well, the boy exploded in anger. "*I am not a **child**!*" he screamed.'

'And then?'

'Nothing! He pedalled off into the gloom. But don't worry. He and his mates'll be back.'

'Thanks for that, Russ,' I said.

We said our goodbyes and I put the phone down.

Thirty years have elapsed since my encounter at Harrow Probation Office with young 'I'm adol' anai.' In the meanwhile, as you can see, nothing, absolutely nothing, has changed.

INTRODUCTION

A SIMPLE APPROACH TO A COMPLEX PROBLEM

Western societies have wrestled with the problem of juvenile delinquency for decades and even in the last two New Labour governments, one of the main political war cries has been: 'Tough on crime, tough on the causes of crime.' But criminologists, politicians, social workers and psychologists have yet to achieve a breakthrough: there is still no real explanation, no viable solution. Ambitiously this book proposes both by considering the reasons behind juvenile delinquency and putting forward recommendations for how to reduce youth crime. The ideas discussed below need to be understood, for if even some of them are accepted and acted upon, the content of children's lives, as well as those of their parents or guardians, will be radically transformed. Simple language, familiar analogy, is therefore vital.

SCALE OF ANTI-SOCIAL BEHAVIOUR – SETTING THE SCENE

Statistics are a morass into which one can easily sink without trace. Nonetheless they are a necessary evil. They help us focus on priorities. One feels that if the same zeal were applied to solving crime as to keeping statistics on it, crime and anti-social behaviour would be a thing of the past. I have tried in this work not to get bogged down in statistics. But sometimes it is unavoidable.

Back in 1991 *Criminal Statistics for England and Wales*, a publication of the UK Government Statistical Service, stated: '...the amount of crime committed is perhaps **three times** the number of crimes recorded by the police' (1991, p. 22). The number of crimes recorded by the police then was 5,276,000. This indicates a total of 15,828,000 crimes, two-thirds of which were unrecorded.

In the next paragraph, one learns...

'Comparison of the BCS (British Crime Survey 1992) estimates of crimes committed with police recorded crimes reveals that there were:

- **twice** as many **domestic burglaries** committed as recorded;
- **more than twice** as many **bicycle thefts;**
- **three** times as many **thefts from vehicles;**
- **four** times as many **woundings;**
- **seven** times as many offences of **vandalism;** and
- **eight** times as many **robberies and thefts from the person**
  (1991, p. 23, bold in original)

And, finally, as if all this were not enough, section 1.20 of the Criminal Statistics provides some, what it calls, 'general' statements:

a) one in three men born in 1953 had been convicted of a serious offence by the age of 30.

b) Most first convictions occurred at age 17; males first convicted in their early teens were more likely to continue offending than those convicted later.

c) Relatively few offenders accounted for a large proportion of convictions; nearly two-thirds of convictions to group a) were committed by the 7 per cent with six or more convictions.

Remember, this latter refers to serious offenders committing *serious* offences.

In 1991, the pie chart of 5,276,000 offences recorded by the police was made up as follows:

Violent crime 5% (263,800);
Criminal damage 16% (844,160);
Burglary 23% (1,213,480);
Other theft 24% (1,266,240);
Car crime 28% (1,477,280);
Fraud and forgery 3% (158,280);
Other 1% (52,760).

We now fast-forward fifteen years to the Home Office Statistical Bulletin, *Crime in England and Wales 2006/07.*

Fifteen years later, the total number of crimes recorded by the police in 2006 has increased (slightly) to 5,428,300 (2007, p. 13).

This makes the key point: in fifteen years, not a lot has changed in England and Wales. Things have not progressed; initiatives have not worked. Perhaps the same can be said not just for this period of fifteen years, but for many decades before this.

The multiplier factor is still present: '... more than half of crimes ... are never reported to the police' (2007, p. 25).

There is little point in burdening the reader with the comparable pie chart for 2006: in April 2002, a new National Crime Recording Standard (NCRS) was introduced. So, unfortunately, the comparison would not be like with like. For example, violent crime which *was* 5% of the 1991 pie chart has shot up to 19% of the 2006 pie chart under the new title of 'violence against the person'.

It still remains the case that most criminal activity is carried out by people of age 30 and under, much of it by youngsters who are still in their teens, and very often early teens.

But this work is not principally about serious crime. It is primarily concerned with juvenile delinquency and anti-social behaviour. This can range from mild fractiousness to, but only in its worst manifestation, outright criminality as represented by some of the figures above.

ARE THE MANY TO 'SUFFER' FOR THE FEW?

It remains the case that many young people make an effortless transition from childhood to adolescence. They do not get into trouble with the Law. Some may become testy and perhaps a little impossible to live, or be, with. But not all these 'angry young men' and increasingly 'angry young women' get into trouble with the Law.

The question is: do these non-criminal youngsters constitute a majority? And, if they do, should they be 'forced' into a time-consuming rite-of-passage programme, such as this book advocates, for the sake of a minority of miscreants?

There are a number of answers to this question:

1) First and foremost, rite of passage is not a punishment. It is a fine process in its own right. One may argue, doubtless everyone will, on the particular pros and cons of this or that rite-of-passage programme; but the principle is right. Our society desperately needs to socialise its young; it desperately needs the innovation of a formal rite of passage.

2) I would like to think that the content of the rite-of-passage programme in Part VIII of this book is sufficiently attractive for most young people to want to participate in it of their own volition.

The programme has certainly not been devised with delinquents or would-be delinquents in mind. It has been devised for all young people irrespective of their behavioural background. This much should quickly become obvious even from the most cursory glance.

3) True, in the suggested rite-of-passage programme in Part VIII, the social pressure to join is overwhelming and the social stigma of not doing so is considerable, but, at the end of the day, participation, so far as this particular programme has been planned, is voluntary.

4) When one takes into account the scale of the 'iceberg' aspect, referred to above, of unreported and therefore unrecorded offences, who is to say that we are not dealing with a majority of young people?

But Don't We Already Have Rites of Passage?

Many people took the view that National Service was a fine rite of passage that created men out of boys. Some people feel that getting a job or becoming a parent is a practical substitute. They are right. But the problem is that these cures, in Western society at least, happen too late.

The Criminal Statistics, quoted above, tells us that 'most first convictions occur at age 17'. By the time young people, particularly young males, get a job or become parents, their lives may already have been blighted. The, I argue, quite natural agitation to leave childhood – and the personal devastation it can cause – can have its beginning as early as eight or ten. One would like to assuage these feelings, this book argues, at a much later age, as late as seventeen; but it seems too difficult to wait even until fourteen. This is the latest age, this book reluctantly suggests, that one can delay the beginning of a rite-of-passage programme.

As things are, getting a job, acquiring a girlfriend, living with a partner, getting married even – these are the palliatives which eventually do calm many 'angry young men' frustrated in their attempts to enter adulthood. This may not happen until a young person's twenties, maybe late twenties. By this time, their lives may well have been unnecessarily but perhaps irrevocably blighted.

Structure of This Book

The book is divided into eight parts.

Part I: The Problem of Transition: identifies in general terms a procedural problem which besets Western society caused by an absence of any rite of passage to embody and externalise the transition between childhood and adulthood.

Part II: The Problem of Antisocial Behaviour explores in more detail how juvenile delinquency, in particular, is a consequence of this lack of a key rite of passage for adolescents.

Part III: The Persistence of Rituals in Society describes the various types of human society, traditional and contemporary, which do not suffer from this problem; explores the extent to which these types of society and ours are mutually compatible; and introduces the anthropological theory behind rite of passage. The next two sections explore the rite-of-passage approach in two contrasting societies.

Part IV: The Maasai Way examines the circumcision rite of the Maasai tribe of Kenya and draws parallels to Western initiation rituals such as those of the Freemasons and the Jewish barmitzvah.

Part V: The Japanese Way explores Japanese culture and concludes that Japan's relatively low youth crime rites are related to the language of Japanese which obliges all its speakers, youth not excluded, to assess deference and respect and act accordingly. Both the Maasai and Japanese cultures have traditionally and successfully transformed their young, in very different ways. Together they provide a framework from which to pick and choose when designing a programme of our own.

Part VI: The Power of Ritual and Myth reviews the meaning and power of ritual and explores different aspects of myth, before positing a contemporary Western myth in which the capricious and dangerous passage of adolescents between childhood and adulthood is dependent on the Destiny. A course of ritual action designed to propitiate Destiny is what is required to transform this into both a myth for our times and a model for exemplary behaviour. The question is: what kind of ritual action would apply to our day and age?

Part VII: The Rite-of-Passage Experience attempts to answer this question from a theoretical point of view by considering the work of Dr David Blumenkrantz's ROPE research project. Blumenkrantz has uniquely applied the idea of rite of passage in a contemporary modern setting and may be considered the father of modern rite of passage.

Finally Part VIII proposes an ambitious rite-of-passage plan, based on the principles discussed hitherto in the book; in this extended section I explore in detail the implications of such a plan and offer some tentative possibilities for the future.

CAUTION

As a philosophical point, everything we have to say stems from the observation that life in Western society would be improved by the introduction of a formal rite of passage to embody and externalise the transition between childhood and adulthood. This is the subject matter of this book. But what if this observation is *wrong*?

The philosopher Bertrand Russell addresses this problem. In fact he characterises it as the principle difference between British and Continental philosophy. In a discussion between the methods of the British philosophers Locke and Hume and the Continental Leibniz he says:

> In Locke or Hume, a comparatively modest conclusion is drawn from a broad survey of many facts, whereas in Leibniz a vast edifice of deduction is pyramided upon a pin-point of logical principle. In Leibniz, if the principle is completely true and the deductions are entirely valid, all is well; but the structure is unstable, and the slightest flaw anywhere brings it down in ruins. In Locke or Hume, on the contrary, the base of the pyramid is on the solid ground of observed fact, and the pyramid tapers upwards not downward; consequently the equilibrium is stable, and a flaw here or there can be rectified without total disaster.
>
> Bertrand Russell, *History of Western Philosophy* (1945, p. 619)

As to the methodology here, you the reader will have to decide. The conclusion that Western society would be improved by the introduction of rite of passage derives from 'a broad survey of many facts'. Hopefully we are putting in place a pyramid with a stable equilibrium which 'tapers upwards not downward'.

Part I

The Problem of Transition

All the world's a stage,
And all the men and women merely players;
They have their exits and their entrances;
And one man in his time plays many parts,
His acts being seven ages:
Shakespeare: *As You Like It* (II: vii)

The Problem of Transition

For this Xhosa boy and many other children in highly ritualised societies, transition is socially organized. In many African cultures, white (clay or chalk) is a symbol of death. This young man will 'die' and 'wake up' a man – that is, if he survives circumcision.

Photography © Ramón Arellano

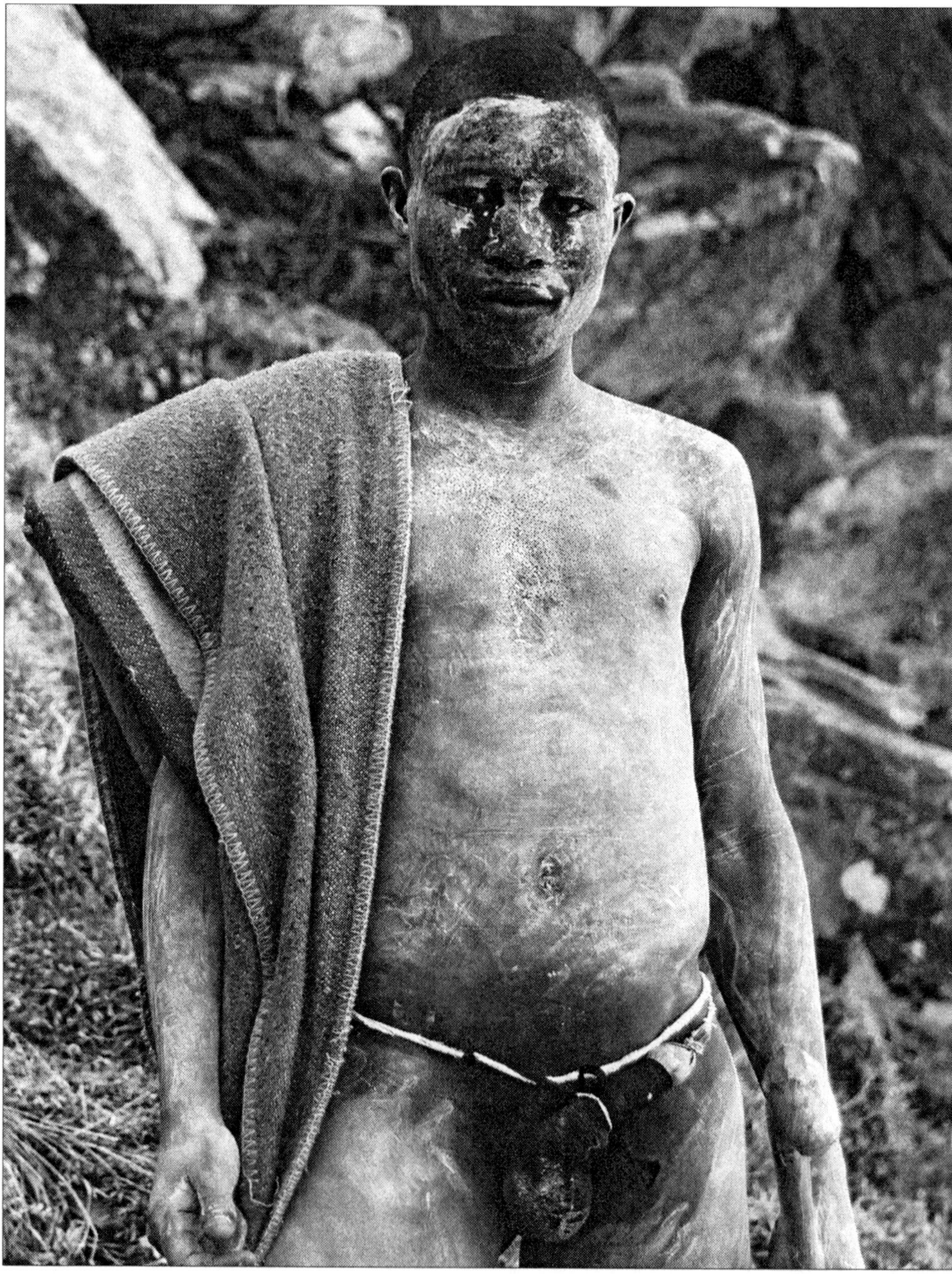

1
The Argument

The argument is this book is that:

1) Antisocial behaviour in young people has a very precise cause.

2) The cause is young people's drive to exit childhood at the earliest opportunity.

3) There is no state-organised programme to accomplish this; there should be.

4) The drive to exit childhood at the earliest opportunity varies from child to child. Some children drift out of childhood effortlessly; many do not.

5) The degree to which each child finds it a problem to exit childhood is the degree to which each child displays antisocial behaviour. This ranges from no antisocial behaviour at all to mild fractiousness to sustained criminality.

6) Those children to whom status-transition is a problem take matters into their own hands in the absence of a state-organised programme. As things stand, they have little alternative.

7) The force behind the drive to exit childhood, the desire for status-transition, is sociological, not psychological.

8) Sociological force produces social pressure. Insofar as a young person reacts at all to this social pressure, he or she may do so individually or as a member of a small informal peer group, often called a gang.

9) The vast majority of young people reacting to the drive to exit childhood are, from a medical point of view, psychologically healthy. The drive to exit childhood is natural and should be seen as such. Antisocial behaviour is an unhealthy reaction to a natural drive.

10) An opportunity to put 'clear blue water' between current perceived status and despised childhood status may be marked by an act of antisocial behaviour.

11) There is a powerful reason why behaviour is frequently *anti*social. Antisocial behaviour most markedly demonstrates departure from childhood norms. Childhood is characterised by conformity and obedience to parental and other social controls.

12) Most acts of antisocial behaviour are to be seen as part of a child's ad hoc, unstructured and opportunistic programme to exit childhood.

13) However not everything that young people do to differentiate themselves from childhood is negative. Voluntary service, particularly voluntary service overseas, as well as gap years at home and abroad, are positive, beneficial and socially approved – and rightly so.

I further argue that:

1) We are dealing with a status-transition problem.

2) This problem has a solution; indeed, more than one.

3) The solution is to be found in highly ritualised societies which are masters of the art of status-transition.

4) In formulating a rite-of-passage programme, our society can adopt the principles of highly ritualised societies and adapt them to our ways.

2
Juvenile Delinquency and Rite of Passage

In principle there are two types of solution to the problem of youth crime. One is the Japanese (or British House of Commons) solution; the other is rite of passage.

The Japanese solution is *very* effective. Antisocial behaviour problems associated with status-transition were minimal in Japan during the latter half of the twentieth century. (Figures substantiating this are included at the end of the book as Appendix 2.) This solution depends upon interlocutors reiterating, and thus reinforcing, each other's status in every sentence uttered. The language of Japanese leaves the speaker of Japanese little choice in the matter. In consequence, everybody knows their place in Japan. This includes ten year olds and teenagers. Status-transition is consequently continuous and automatic.

Translating the Japanese model to Western shores is culturally impossible. This must be obvious. The degree to which the Japanese people and the Japanese language pay regard to hierarchy and deference is too great for us to begin to emulate – except, as mentioned, in the British House of Commons! In short, Japanese practice can't be adapted to our culture. I therefore advocate rite of passage, which is a process we can adapt.

Note

An attempt at contemporary rite of passage has been made. It's wrong to say the attempt has failed, but equally it hasn't fully succeeded. This fascinating experiment is covered in Part VII.

Suffice to say at this introductory stage, for rite of passage to succeed three fundamental conditions must be fulfilled:

1) There must be ritual in the rite-of-passage process.
2) Rite of passage must govern *all* children in the land, from prince to pauper.

3) There must be 'passage'. This means there must be transition from one formal and defined status (child) to another formal and defined status (young adult).

Any rite of passage ignoring these criteria, even one of them, will fail. It will not be a true rite of passage. On the other hand, a rite of passage which embodies these criteria will succeed.

TWO RITES OF PASSAGE

It is possible to think of *two* rites of passage. Creating and overseeing a rite-of-passage programme will in itself be a rite of passage – for the state! The road from where the state is now to where it needs to be to launch a rite-of-passage programme will be long and hard. 'Passage' – as in rite of passage – will not be easy. The state, backed by public opinion, may very well come to the conclusion that the status quo, with all its drawbacks, will seem preferable to all changes that need to be made to alter it.

A viable rite-of-passage programme, as you will discover, cannot be put in place tomorrow morning. There will be law to be changed – lots of it. And who knows how much will fail in the Court of Public Opinion?

My main fear is that the government of the day will treat rite of passage as a buzzword, under whose umbrella one half-baked programme after another will be launched. The result is predictable – unabated anti-social behaviour or continuing 'crimes of passage'.

Remember, for a rite of passage to be a rite of passage and for status-transition to be possible, each one of the three criteria mentioned above *must* be present.

POLICY AND INPUT

This work investigates rite of passage which is the time-honoured way by which human beings move from one status to another. Any wedding you have attended will have been a rite of passage for the bride and groom. It just happens that it's not yet in our tradition to hold a ceremony to move a child on to the next stage of his or her life. I hope that instituting such a ceremony will become policy. This book is therefore intended to interest policy-makers, anyone involved with youth, a phrase to be construed liberally. It ranges from those carrying ministerial responsibility for youth to every father and mother without exception. No-one is immune from the distress of antisocial behaviour.

Rite of passage offers a glittering opportunity. Provided it is presented properly, it offers young people the chance to discover themselves in a positive way and to blossom into adolescence and adulthood. The more a rite-of-passage programme demands from young people, the more they will respond. If the Establishment grows wise, it can harness the burgeoning power of youth for the benefit of all. Powerful anti-Establishment antisocial behaviour can be turned round. It can be done and this is a heady prospect.

3
All the World's a Stage

A Theatrical Analogy

We have a procedural problem in how we live. Our society has no effective means of providing young people with a formal enactment, or rite of passage, to mark the transition between childhood and adulthood; as a result children appear to behave prematurely like adults, and equally adults appear to behave like children, long after the supposed age of maturity. For most young people the boundaries between the two states, childhood and adulthood, are not just uncertain but nonexistent, and every teenager, boy and girl, is left to cross the minefield of adolescence without a map, a compass, or any mental armour against 'the slings and arrows of outrageous fortune' in their entrance to the world of adults. This defective state can best be expressed by another metaphor, also from Shakespeare, who highlighted the human lifespan by using a *theatrical* analogy. In *As You Like It* (Act II, vii), in less than thirty lines, Shakespeare considers human life as embodying seven ages with life first being seen as a 'great play':

> All the world's a stage,
> And all the men and women merely players;

Participation in the 'play' is automatic; involvement is *de facto*, conferred by birth; and fate arbitrarily arranges the roles that men and women play.

> They have their exits and their entrances;
> And one man in his time plays many parts,
> His acts being seven ages.

This implies that just as there are exits and entrances to and from the theatrical stage, from one scene to another, there are, similarly, exits and entrances from one act of life to another. The idea of exits and entrances is therefore *not* new thinking and there is no new concept to be grasped here.

If the idea of exits and entrances from one stage of life to another has been with us since Shakespeare's time, the actual practice of exits and entrances has been enacted in certain human societies from time immemorial. Some human societies still make provision and practise this, but Western society does not – with devastating consequences. It has forgotten the importance of exits and entrances from one social life stage to another. Western society must gain or regain this awareness.

Returning to Shakespeare's lines, one can identify the precise point where juvenile delinquent behaviour begins:

> At first the infant,
> Mewling and puking in the nurse's arms;
> Then the whining school-boy, with his satchel
> And shining morning face, creeping like a snail
> Unwillingly to school. And then the lover,

In this last line, the switch from 'Unwillingly to school' to 'And then the lover', suggests an apparently effortless transition from one role to another. Unfortunately such a transition is usually anything but effortless. The 'And then' is *our* problem. *We* have to develop a script for 'entrance' to Shakespeare's 'act three'. In modern life we are referring to the adolescent years.

Maintaining the 'theatre of life' analogy, delinquent behaviour will break out, if it's going to, when exit and, in particular, entrance is ignored. In theatrical terms, it's all about theatre direction and stage management. But in Western society, there is no formal exit strategy for the end of act two, the schoolchild period; and there is no formal entrance strategy for the beginning of the third act of life and whatever roles come with it.

4
Juvenile Delinquency and Status Change

It's a jungle out there

If there is no formal exit/entrance strategy, there's certainly an informal one; and delinquent behaviour is the signature of the informal strategy that adolescents devise. Without a state-sponsored 'drama school', juveniles prepare for role-change as best they can on an individual basis. It's everyone for himself – and, increasingly, herself.

Adolescents engage in behaviour which, from an adult's point of view, is spontaneous, ad hoc, ill-tempered, bad-mannered, usually irresponsible and frequently illegal. You can probably think of more adjectives to add to the stream. If parents or guardians are lucky, the ad hoc programme will express itself in a period of mild fractiousness; if unlucky, of sustained criminality. From the adolescent's point of view, such behaviour is often fun and adventurous. It is behaviour that is also, somewhat strangely, 'natural' and 'driven'. Any transition from one life stage to another involves a change in personal status. This change has to be *managed*. Without proper management, the change in personal status may be inconclusive, which leads to anger and frustration.

Transition from adolescence to young adulthood is particularly fraught. One reason for this is obvious: adolescents are at the peak of good health and strength; added to this that they are frequently inarticulate and it's readily understandable that feelings of frustration and anger are vented in a physical and bad-tempered way. So, to repeat, the phenomenon of juvenile delinquency is to be understood as what can happen when the time for change in personal status is totally mismanaged or, most usually, not managed at all. In the absence of any official programme organised by the state, each child feels mysteriously coerced into acting out his or her own ad hoc 'change-in-personal-status' programme.

THE STATE'S POSITION

The exit from childhood's act two to young adult act three is unscripted. Will the state provide a script? Or shall we continue to leave it to the children themselves?

As things are, the state doesn't organise exits and entrances. The state sees the issue from its own legal and administrative point of view. It recognises the need for transition and has opted for the age of 18 to mark transition from minor to major: at the stroke of midnight on an adolescent's 18th birthday, the state recognises instant transition to legally responsible adult individual.

Objectively, this may be very convenient; unfortunately, it's totally lost on the teenager. He, or she, doesn't experience any particular feeling of change. From an adolescent's point of view, turning 18 is a casual milestone of no particular significance. Seventeen was also a milestone; it was possible then to apply for a driving licence and drive on the roads on passing the test. Sixteen was a milestone: it was possible to enter the armed forces. It was also possible to obtain for the first time one's own individual ten-year passport.

How many milestones can there be?

None of these milestones gives any official indication of changed personal status. They may to an adult; but they don't to an adolescent. Any of these *could* constitute an 'entrance'. But dished out in such a matter-of-fact, piecemeal and casual way, they're supremely untheatrical. Consequently they pass unrecognised and are afforded no special significance.

TEST

Is personal status *per se* really the issue? Here's a simple test. Ask any teenager: 'Do you think adulthood comes *automatically* by just *waiting* until you reach a certain age? Yes or no?'

If you get the answer *Yes*, ask the teenager what that age is; and why?

It can confidently be predicted that eight out of every ten teenagers will answer in the negative – namely, that adulthood does *not* happen 'automatically'. That was certainly so when this question was part of a questionnaire submitted in 1995 to young offenders in young offender institutions and also to boys and girls in state and public schools (see Appendix 1). The percentage for boys, girls and young offenders never varied: only two from ten thought adulthood *did* come automatically.

With eight out of ten taking the view they do, it's no wonder adolescents take a *pro*active rather than a *re*active approach to the issue.

Adulthood is something you just can't hang around waiting for to happen. If you're a teenager, it's in *your* hands. It's up to *you* to start the ball rolling. To *do* something! The question is *what?*

Part II

The Problem of Antisocial Behaviour

The Problem of Anti-social Behaviour

Alcohol, drugs, 'joy riding' – the calculated departure from childhood norms can sometimes be miscalculated and get totally out of control.

Photography: Alain Juteau

5

THE CAUSES OF ANTISOCIAL BEHAVIOUR

DRACONIAN LAW

Before considering what adolescents do, it is worth noting that adolescent misbehaviour is not always a permanent fact of life. There are conditions in which misbehaviour is subdued, if not totally sublimated. In dictatorships where the law is draconian, delinquency will be diminished. If the punishment for theft is the loss of a limb, a potential thief is obviously going to think twice before going into action. The risk involved isn't worth it, especially if the theft, as is frequently the case, is more motivated by the bravado of the act of theft itself than by any importance attached to the intrinsic value of the item/s stolen.

There will be those who applaud draconian laws, but they should be wary of doing so as the price paid is too great. Draconian law, apart from being arbitrary, is all-pervasive. Regimes extend their total control to music and art, politics, religion and science. Such an approach to the control of crime is flawed, unnecessary and counter-productive. Juvenile misbehaviour does, admittedly, decline in conditions of grinding poverty, because in such conditions, criminality is unlikely to be gratuitous. Life itself becomes a battle for survival among young and old alike. Theft, particularly the theft of food, is understandable if not excusable.

But our society is not draconian. Nor, fortunately, is it burdened with grinding poverty. Quite the opposite. The antics of the young seem all the more incomprehensible in that they are played out in conditions of superabundance and *embarras de richesse*. In fact, wealth itself fuels juvenile misbehaviour. In conditions of wealth juveniles have *time*. They have the time to perceive that nothing is happening in their lives. There should be change and there isn't.

Insofar as society positively *does* take an interest in a juvenile's progress, it limits its interest to a child's educational achievement.

BAD BEHAVIOUR

Why do adolescents exhibit behaviour that is frequently antisocial, negative and destructive? Not all youngsters behave badly; some make the transition to young adult status without trauma, but an enormous number do get into trouble. Maintaining the theatrical analogy, bad behaviour undoubtedly makes for better theatre. Bad behaviour makes 'exit' more decisive and 'entrance' more dramatic. With bad behaviour, exit from the schoolchild role will be overt, pronounced, demonstrable and final. This childhood role can be characterised as passive obedience to parent/s and teachers.

This public display of departure from previous norms indicates readiness for 'entrance' to a new status – and, indeed, the public display of departure from previous norms *is* in itself a mark of that new status. And if the new status is lived out for a few months or years even in the cell of a young offenders institution, this is in itself public proclamation of social transition. In certain social groups, incarceration is a considerable badge of honour!

But it would be a mistake to believe that we are dealing with gifted thespians. Delinquency reflects genuine anger and frustration. The source of the anger and frustration is generally totally unknown to the delinquent. As with any form of pain, reaction is in no way modified by ignorance of its source. If anything, it is exacerbated.

It's always easier to reproduce antisocial behaviour than its opposite: it is hard to be a hero! How often is one afforded the opportunity in life to play the role of hero? Not often, if at all. One can't go out onto the street and expect to rescue a child, or an old lady, from the path of a ten-ton out-of-control lorry. But the opportunity to steal a handbag or throw a brick through a window is ever-present.

The very last thing most adolescents *want* is to receive accolades from the Establishment. Such accolades are bad for street-cred!

CHAPMAN'S 'DIFFERENT BREED OF CAT'

Chapman (1968) has produced a full list of psychological manoeuvres and stratagems by which men, women and children interact. Juvenile delinquency and adolescent misbehaviour are entertainingly treated, with devastating insight, in a three-page narrative labelled: 'Different Breed of Cat'.

> In the stratagem of Different Breed of Cat, which is executed mainly by adolescents, the teenager seeks to establish his independence and individuality by developing customs, standards and behaviour which are strikingly different from

> those of this parents; it is a classic kind of put-off stratagem. To a certain extent, a majority of adolescents carry out mild stratagems of Different Breed of Cat. The boys let their hair grow long and the girls wear their skirts very short. Adolescents carry out mild varieties of Different Breed of Cat in clothing, grooming, speech idioms and the way they entertain themselves. (p. 63)

Chapman continues:

> However, the stratagem of Different Breed of Cat becomes serious when it results in a full-scale rebellion of the adolescent against the standards and customs of his parents. When carried to extremes, Different Breed of Cat leads businessmen's sons to rob filling stations and ministers' daughters to become sexually promiscuous. (p. 64)

Chapman describes a boy whose parents concentrated on their public careers to his detriment. The boy repaid their lack of attention to him by getting into serious police trouble. Initially, their influence ensured only moderate penalties for his misbehaviour, but ultimately his crimes became too serious to be ignored. He was sentenced to two years' imprisonment in a high-security prison. His parents felt, and were, socially disgraced. The boy had secured his 'revenge'; and blighted his life in the process.

As a psychiatrist, Chapman, not unreasonably, tends to see things in psychological terms. Although the psychological dimension cannot be ignored, and some case-histories present an obvious psychological aspect, I believe the Different Breed of Cat stratagem to be a sociological rather than a psychological phenomenon. In support of this contention and to re-quote Chapman as cited above:

> To a certain extent, a *majority of adolescents* [my emphasis] carry out mild stratagems of Different Breed of Cat.

Chapman concludes on a brighter note:

> However, the end result of Different Breed of Cat usually is less serious: the stratagem may even be amusing to the uninvolved spectator although the participants usually go through a fair amount of misery. In fact most stratagems of Different Breed of Cat are self-limiting; the adolescent establishes his triumphant individuality, he no longer needs the stratagem, and he drops it.
>
> I recall a seventeen year old girl who flourished a long cigarette holder before her bewildered parents as she talked of 'the sexual revolution', 'the stodginess of virginity', and the advisability of 'frequent trial marriages' beginning in

> mid-adolescence. She often brought these topics up before her parents' friends, and remonstrances from her parents evoked a smile of pity from her as she patronisingly chided them for their 'hopelessly outdated ideas and customs'. After several years of tormenting her parents and flaunting her individuality, she gave up this masquerade and settled down to a sedate suburban life. Her parents are waiting with undisguised vengeful anticipation for the day when the girl's children begin their own adolescent stratagems of Different Breed of Cat.

Echoing Chapman's observations, the following e-mail joke is currently doing the rounds. A teenaged boy with spiked hair, nose-ring and baggy clothes is overheard telling a friend: 'I don't really like to dress like this, but it keeps my parents from dragging me everywhere with them.'

6
DESTINY TESTING

The absence of a state-run programme for child-to-adult status-change imposes an additional problem upon the child. In playing out his or her own programme, there is no formal way to tell *when* entrance to new status has finally been achieved. Adolescent misbehaviour continues – escalates even. There's no-one to say 'enough's enough'.

For some adolescents the desire to metamorphose from child to young adult runs *very* deep. In some societies, as we shall see, young men die from the physical ordeal their society imposes upon them at the time of transition change. Death is accepted and the publicly held view is that the youngster who has succumbed was never *destined* to achieve full manhood.

One of these deeds of derring-do is joyriding – jumping into (usually stolen) cars and careering round at high speeds. But the term *joy*riding is of course a complete misnomer. It totally fails to convey the motivation for the escapade. The phenomenon should more accurately be termed *destiny testing*.

Joyriding is a desperate attempt at status change and appeals especially to those who question in their deepest psyche whether they will ever turn adult. These are youngsters who harbour the underlying feeling they may never be *destined* to do so. Taking life-threatening chances, dicing with death, is their way of finding out. For many youngsters it's their *only* way of finding out. The problem for the joyrider is, as mentioned above, there's no-one to tell him when he's 'done enough'. If he's managed to 'drive and survive' at 70 mph, maybe, he continues to think to himself, the *real* test is to try to do so at 80, 90 or 100 mph. Each successful escapade is merely an entrance ticket to another, even more dangerous.

There is an intermediate state between life and death: severe injury. This 'half-death' gives its crippled victims a whole lifetime to ponder the folly of an immature and self-prescribed attempt to reach maturity in a society that provided no official lead or direction.

There has to be a better way.

DRUGS TOO ARE DESTINY TESTING

Joyriding is by no means the only example of destiny testing. The decision to take drugs is frequently similarly motivated. Most drugs are certainly not as death-defying as joyriding; risk is modified by personal control over dosage. But insofar as there *is* risk, to both body and mind, drugs are destiny testing, even if only symbolically. In the personal decision to move into drugs, a juvenile exits from childhood status, in his or her own eyes at least, and those of the peer group.

It cannot be denied that young people may be attracted to the risk element of drug-taking and when the authorities highlight the danger of taking drugs, they only serve to accentuate children's interest, while school awareness campaigns on the danger of drugs tend to have precisely the opposite effect to that intended. A child's 'exit' strategy from childhood status is dictated by risk and danger rather than health and safety.

There are a few adolescents, an annually growing number, upon whom despair descends: these are victims of the perception that they are 'time-warped' by continuous never-ending childhood and non-adult status. In their own minds, they have 'failed', but they're probably not quite sure exactly how they've failed. From their point of view, they are 'drifting' through teens and twenties as overgrown schoolchildren in some sort of netherworld. Whatever it is they are required to do to change their fate is beyond them. They have become terminally confused and don't know any longer which question, or questions, to ask. Such feelings are the principal reason behind an adolescent's awesome decision to take destiny into their own hands and finalise its outcome, by committing suicide.

7
Education and Socialisation

The question inevitably arises: how has our sophisticated Western society failed to recognise the importance of planned child-to-adult transition? How have we overlooked the importance of exit and entrance-ing? The answer is that Western society has invested its all in education. 'Education, education, education' has been the hallmark of government commitment towards youth. Nor should this vision be criticised. Education is the bed-rock, the sine qua non, of any sophisticated modern civilised society.

Unfortunately, this instillation of knowledge hardly seems to stave off the puzzling propensity of adolescents to engage in antisocial behaviour; the problem is that education, per se, is not enough. Education is essentially intellectual and transition from one status to another is definitely not an intellectual but a social process. Western society has confused the two: education and socialisation. Education is cerebral; socialisation is not. Socialisation is all about status recognition, role performance and status change. Education is tested by examination; socialisation by public and peer group appreciation.

Socialisation into life-beyond-school is not a matter of intelligence. It's as equally binding on the intelligent and unintelligent alike. Nor is it a matter of wealth or social class: prince and pauper are equally bound by the same social imperative. Society, government, parents, children themselves even, may hope that socialisation for life-beyond-school will be an automatic by-product of the educational process. This is understandable; one can see why this might be so. Unfortunately, the two are different. The one (socialisation) is rarely found subsumed within the other.

8
THE AGE OF MATURITY

ENTRANCE AT 35

IN JUNE 2003, there were a number of articles in British newspapers about the results of a recent study suggesting that men eventually mature at the age of 35 while women do so five years earlier. These statistics may or may not be true but they do highlight two important points: first, that juveniles do eventually mature and secondly that, except in relatively few cases, juveniles are not career criminals. Juvenile delinquency, adolescent misbehaviour, is a means to an end, not an end in itself.

This leads to a further observation: the delinquent adolescent is worthy of sympathy. Adolescent misbehaviour is governed by forces at work upon the adolescent for which he or she has no awareness and consequently no ability to control. Sympathy, though, is sometimes very hard to find: delinquent behaviour is often just too outrageous. Time spent on sympathy is time wasted. Such time is better spent on seeking a solution to the juvenile's predicament. Success promises rich reward: the prospect of a cadre of youth whose lives are unblighted and whose integration into mainstream society has been achieved without undue trauma.

MAKING MEN OUT OF BOYS

There certainly have been times when the exigencies of life rendered the need for any special socialisation programme totally unnecessary. For example, in time of war, exit from school was often followed by entrance to the army. Army experience made 'men out of boys'. But today we live in an age of potential push-button mass destruction. Conscription is not a realistic military option. But that is secondary to the main point that it was the army not the school that made 'men out of boys'. Today there is no natural follow-on, no army Act III to school's Act II. Compounding the problem today are the twin sirens for young people of having too much spare time and too much money; both of which beguile them into their nihilistic snare.

As a result the state must take on additional responsibility. The state, as if it already didn't have enough to do, must organise and oversee the conversion of adolescents into young adults. The process is too important to leave to youngsters themselves. The transition is, anyhow, as we have tried to show, one which most adolescents can sometimes mismanage when left to their own devices. This much, society knows to its own cost.

SENIOR CITIZENS OUT OF MEN

If the cause of juvenile delinquency is the failure to arrange proper exit-and-entrancing from schooldays to life beyond, there is one lifestage transition in particular that is mismanaged, Shakespeare's sixth age.

> The sixth age shifts
> Into the lean and slipper'd pantaloon
> With spectacles on nose and pouch on side,
> His youthful hose, well sav'd, a world too wide
> For his shrunk shank; and his big manly voice,
> Turning again towards childish treble, pipes
> And whistles in his sound.

Job exit followed by entrance-into-retirement is a very serious business. Failure to handle it properly frequently results in premature death, not necessarily *at* the time of retirement but not too long afterwards; perhaps within two or three years.

Ostensibly, there is clear medical cause of death: heart attack or cancer. And few people are in a position, or would have any inclination, to gainsay the medical verdict. But the real cause of death is not medical but social: loss of role, too sudden cut-off from previous position, status and authority. These are the real killers that forestall transition to 'the lean and slipper'd pantaloon'. The author, Martin Page calls it 'sudden expulsion from the tribe'. The 'tribe' in this case is previous professional or company employment:

> It can euphemistically be called 'declaring redundant' or 'retiring early', but if the circumstances are the same, so is the prospect of fatal consequences.
>
> Page, *The Company Savage*, op. cit., p. 47

The contrast between the reaction of young and old to mismanaged exit-and-entrancing could not be greater. The young display anything from mild fractiousness (rare) to outrageous misbehaviour (common); the older generation conduct themselves with forlorn and passive acceptance. They can't cause trouble; they don't and won't fill the courts or prisons. There will be no call for 'old offender institutions'. They will lie down and quietly die of a broken heart. In short, their plight can be, and more often than not is, ignored! 'Role maketh the man,' it is said. But, no role, and in no time at all, no man!

The plight of the retiree is further compounded: a proportion will come to the end of their natural lifespan towards the end of their sixth or seventh decade. Who is to say who has died from a broken heart and who hasn't? Transition to senior citizen status is frequently mismanaged, but proposals for a solution must be the subject of another study.

Part III

The Persistence of Rituals in Society

The Persistence of Ritual in Society

In Western society ritual is alive and well, especially among the great and the good. Mr Speaker Martin and his retinue lead Right Honourable and Honourable Gentleman from the House of Commons (a very 'Japanese institution') through to the House of Lords to listen to the Queen's speech from the throne.

Photography: Deryc Sands. This image is covered by UK Parliamentary copyright and is reproduced with the permission of Parliament.

9
From Entertainment to Ritual Drama

'All the world's a stage', has been a perfect analogy in considering the development stages of human life in theatrical terms. Yet this analogy doesn't quite go far enough for our purposes. However profound the implications of Shakespeare's works, his primary aim was to entertain rather than reform.

There are two kinds of theatre: entertainment theatre and ritual drama. In the former a company of artists put on a play for entertainment purposes, usually for gain, to be performed to successive audiences for as long as possible. The latter, on the other hand, is most unlikely to be performed to paying guests or to successive audiences, and the audience as well as the actors are, as often as not, members of the cast. If the former provides entertainment, the latter provides change – of the world or any aspect of it; above all, change, alteration or adjustment in the personal status of an individual or group of individuals, in their position in the world.

A perfect example of ritual drama with which most people will be familiar would be a religious wedding service: a one-off event at the conclusion of which a man and a woman are changed in status and transformed into husband and wife in front of witnesses. A religious service is not performed for entertainment purposes; it is not entertainment theatre, but is performed for ritual purposes. True, the service may display theatrical aspects: distinctive costume, music, song and dance, feasting or fasting. The content of ritualised human behaviour is, after all, as varied as life itself. There may even be individuals whose background role is to mastermind choreography, to direct operations. But, theatrical as this may seem to an outside observer, this is not a theatrical performance. It is solemn activity for a specific purpose. A religious service is a ritual act.

Many who have observed ritualised behaviour have misled themselves into believing they were watching simple entertainment theatre. In the words of J.S. La Fontaine, a professional student of human culture:

> ritual, unlike a play, is purposeful activity: that is, it aims to affect the world. [...] Whether it is the material world that is to be affected, as in the rituals for rain, at harvest or when bringing new ground under cultivation, or human beings who are to be redistributed among the groups that make up social life, ritual is expected to produce results. The performance is not an end in itself but a means to achieve other ends. The analogy with the theatre brings out certain qualities of initiation rites but it does not get us very far.
>
> La Fontaine, *Initiation, Ritual Drama and Secret Knowledge across the World*, p. 184

THE POWER OF RITUAL DRAMA

To reiterate:

> ritual, unlike a play, is purposeful activity: that is, it aims to affect the world [...] ritual is expected to *produce results*' (my italics).

Ritual, then, exerts power over people, a power deriving from the performance of a socially prescribed act or acts. As long as these acts are socially prescribed it really doesn't matter what they are. Belief in their efficacy is entirely subjective. But, as long as *everybody* believes, that's good enough. Ritual acts are rather like Humpty-Dumpty's words:

> 'When I use a word' Humpty-Dumpty said in a rather scornful tone, 'it means just what I choose it to mean – neither more nor less.'
>
> Lewis Carroll, *Through the Looking-Glass*

In other words, the form and content of a ritual may be anything you like (though as we shall see in Part IV, rituals the world over tend to have a defined form), but so long as every participant and witness to the performance of the drama agrees with the purpose and social objective of the ritual activity, then the outcome will be exactly as desired. In a ritual context, exit-and-entrancing can therefore be achieved in an infinite variety of ways.

Let us not forget these words: *purposeful* activity; aims to *affect* the world; expected to *produce results;* not an end in itself, but a *means* to achieve *other ends.*

La Fontaine relates a story from her research:

I well remember the eager questions of two Herero men [a people of Namibia and Botswana] who, on hearing that I was writing a book on initiation, demanded that I explain what they had always wondered about. It seems that they had a playmate, a girl of their own age, who was a good friend and joined in all their games, 'like a boy'. Then she was taken off to the girls' initiation rite, and afterwards 'she was not the same'. She did not wish to associate with them, nor join in their games; she even spoke and behaved differently. They wanted to know what could explain this. The ritual experience had changed her: she had become a woman and they were still little boys.

La Fontaine, op. cit., p. 185

10
Western Ritual

There are societies that successfully mature their youth, which are highly ritualised societies. It is tempting to protest that, as Western society is definitely not highly ritualised, to apply any scheme based on the performance of ritual to our society must be dead in the water before it starts. However, this is not necessarily the case.

First, people in Western society are just as capable of behaving ritualistically as those in non-Western societies. The human mind is universal. Secondly, contrary to what might be expected, not only are Westerners capable of behaving as ritualistically as their non-Western counterparts, but in Western reality they actually do behave just as ritualistically. The problem is we can't see the wood for the trees.

The word 'ritual' is concisely defined as:

> 1. a prescribed order of performing rites.
> 2. a procedure regularly followed.
>
> *Concise Oxford Dictionary*, 10th edition, 1998 p. 1189

Taking the second definition, the daily greeting is a ritual most people observe. The following story – of a researcher who wanted to find out what happened if the social nicety of the daily greeting were not to be observed – may be apocryphal. It's something you can try yourself, but be warned: you proceed at your peril!

The researcher marched into work for a couple of weeks and went 'straight into the day' without saying good morning to his secretary. The atmosphere immediately deteriorated. The poor lady thought she'd committed some awful sin. When eventually he called off the 'experiment' there was palpable relief – plus a great deal of recrimination assuaged by flowers and chocolates.

'A procedure regularly followed' could apply in Western society to so many things – dress code, presentation of food, terms of address – we exhibit ritual behaviour in every area of life. What we regard as meaningless mumbo-jumbo in other cultures is normal and unremarkable in our own: our forms of speech and the prescribed occasions on which we use them; our forms of dress and the prescribed occasions on which we wear them; our food and the prescribed occasions on which we eat it and so on. Our culture is sacrosanct. Our way of doing things is completely normal. It's everybody else that's mad!

THE GREAT, THE GOOD AND THE JUST

Although Western man is prey to countless rituals they may not appear to be exotic in the sense that older or more technologically 'primitive' societies, such as those of African, South American or Australian aboriginal cultures can seem to be, especially as portrayed in films. In fact, however, Western man behaves just as exotically as his African, South American or Australian counterparts. To take three examples from all sections of the class spectrum, the rituals performed by football fans and Freemasons in the UK and the Bonesmen in the United States, are deeply embedded in their respective cultures and to a Martian would appear every bit as exotic as those of highly ritualised societies.

THE FANS

Marsh, Rosser and Harre in *The Rules of Disorder* researched the behaviour of football fan supporters of Oxford United FC. 'Life on the Terraces' (Marsh *et al.*, 1978, ch. 3) relates ritual behaviour paralleling anything you might see among warring New Guinea tribes. Similarities in ritual between those of our society and more technologically primitive societies are, if anything, closer in the 2000s than they were in the 1970s; for instance, facial body painting was uncommon in the 1970s but was prevalent during the 2006 World Cup in Germany.

Little has changed otherwise. The full panoply of football fan roles still exists: Organiser, Chant Leader, 'Aggro' Leader, Hooligan, Nutter and Scapegoat – all of whom can be seen to discharge structured roles. The average football fan would probably suss out quicker than most, and enjoy, what was going on in a bout of traditional and ritual New Guinea tribal warfare. Like a football match, the event is a good day out. Unlike a football match no-one is allowed to win! A very few people, it's true, do get hurt, but this serves to inject the event with authenticity!

THE MASONS

Freemasonry prides itself on secrecy. It recruits its members from all walks of life – including the aristocracy. At the time of writing, a prominent member of the Royal Family is Grand Master of the United Grand Lodge of England. Members of all professions adorn the ranks of the Brotherhood.

Freemasonry's ritual is very dramatic. Props for initiation, for example, include a blindfold, a noose and a dagger. The candidate to be initiated will be paraded blindfolded around the Lodge, his trouser-leg rolled up, a shoe on one foot and a slipper on the other. The 'audience' are wearing lambskin aprons and address each other formally according to title. The ceremony is designed to be – and is – a dramatic occasion. For most candidates, involvement will be memorable: the startling recognition of familiar faces in unfamiliar roles; a dramatic introduction into a new world of hierarchical relationships.

People from all walks of life – judges, generals, businessmen – patronise the ranks of Freemasonry. Everyone who has joined The Brotherhood *must* be familiar with the ritual drama of Freemasonry's initiation ceremony. Those who perpetuate their interest in Freemasonry will witness and perform more. If the great, the good and the just in Western society find it in themselves to participate in the performance of bizarre ritual drama, albeit behind closed doors – so can everybody else.

Once again, we should remind ourselves of La Fontaine's words (cited above): we are dealing in Freemasonry ritual, as in every other ritual, with 'purposeful activity'; activity which 'aims to affect the world'; which is 'expected to produce results'; and, above all, 'performance (which) is not an end in itself but a means to achieve other ends'. Theatrical as it all is, this is not a piece of entertainment theatre. Fascinating as it is, Freemasonry's core raison d'être is another subject.

One might wish to disassociate oneself from involvement in, and performance of, ritual drama on the grounds that it's all too bizarre and ridiculous. A particular rite, or series of rites, may appear that way, for sure. There are powerful reasons *why* rituals, particularly *transition* rituals – that is, rituals designed to project a human being from one social status to another – are bizarre, dramatic and, very frequently, apparently dangerous or actually dangerous.

But one would be ill-advised to concentrate too much upon the form or content of ritual; rather, one should consider its social objective. If, having made this consideration, one still declines involvement, participation and performance, then so be it. This must always be an option in a free society.

But then equally it's fair for the free society reciprocally to decline to confer the benefits of the social objective – and in the context of this study, it's the social objective of full adult status – upon anyone who contracts out. This would certainly apply to adolescents who decline to involve themselves in a status transition programme. They would pay a heavy price: exit from childhood would remain formally unachieved; entrance to adulthood equally so.

THE BONESMEN

The performance of secret exotic rites is by no means limited to Masonic ritual. Many professions indulge in secret initiation rituals. American universities in particular sanction such rituals for their students. The Skull and Bones Society at Yale University is a case in point.

This society is elite. It is male-only and admits a mere 15 members a year. Many of the 800 or so living associates occupy leading roles in American society. The contenders for the 2004 Presidential election were both themselves Bonesmen: the incumbent President George W. Bush and his then opponent Senator John Kerry of Massachusetts.

Both men will have undergone the Skull and Bones society initiation rites. These rites are performed at a Greco-Egyptian temple located at the Yale university campus. The temple is said to contain a host of relics including silver from Hitler's hoard and the skull of the famous American Indian Chief, Geronimo. Initiation rites are said to include mud-wrestling sessions, beatings, and recitation of personal sexual history while lying naked in a coffin. This sexual history, it seems, may be immediately developed by the ritual presence of a resident prostitute!

Alexandra Robbins, herself a Yale graduate, has written of the Skull and Bones Society in her book *Secrets of the Tomb*. Once again, we see the performance of, and submission to, ritual drama as being almost a sine qua non for propulsion into position, and sometimes, very high position. It's all too easy to sit back and imagine the scenes enacted at the Skull and Bones Society and think how ridiculous and licentious they are. But that is to miss the point. Ritual drama is purposeful activity. Transition to new status depends on the performance of prescribed ritual acts. What these acts are hardly matters. The ritual drama, in the case of the Bonesmen, comprises pleasant and unpleasant experiences. But if you wish to be initiated into this small and elite fellowship, you engage in the time-honoured ritual, without question. The same applies to any group: insofar as ritual drama is time-honoured, who is entitled to question the prescribed rites?

The performance of ritual drama is the means by which, perhaps the *only* means by which, human beings are linked to their social past, re-adjusted within their social present, and directed to their social future. An individual whose life is bereft of ritual is greatly to be pitied. In Western society, we look on as helpless spectators, as so many, if not most, of today's adolescents mindlessly rampage through their teenage years in an ad hoc, spontaneous and undirected way. Our task, our duty, is to provide direction as quickly as possible.

11
Western vs Highly Ritualised Societies

Western and highly ritualised societies are to be contrasted by the degree to which participation in ritual drama is culturally determined. If Westerners are as capable as their non-Western counterpart of performing ritual drama, it nevertheless remains the case that, in Western society, participation is largely, if not entirely, voluntary. This state of affairs is not to be decried. It underpins freedom. Our freedom, within the law, to choose to take part in a social activity or not is a vital privilege, to be jealously guarded.

However Western society is currently faced with an acute procedural problem: its failure to provide an exit–and-entrance strategy for smooth social transition from life's Act II to life's Act III (that is, the period beyond primary school), which must be addressed as soon as possible. Western legislature and public opinion will debate the extent to which it is fair to compel participation, which in turn will depend on the nature of the proposals put forward. In highly ritualised societies, ability to opt out is extremely limited. Indeed one definition of a highly ritualised society is that involvement in, and performance of, its cultural ritual drama is, for the most part, an all-embracing imperative.

Highly ritualised societies: low and high technology

Many people will associate highly ritualised societies with the word *primitive* and could hardly be blamed for doing so. Many highly ritualised societies *are* primitive. However, before adopting this pejorative label, the limitation within which the word 'primitive' is justifiable must be put into context. This context is actually very limited. The term 'primitive' has possible meaning only when associated with technology. In all other respects, its use is incorrect.

The majority of highly ritualised societies do display low levels of technological accomplishment. It is also true that Western societies, swelling in pride at their own high level of technological accomplishment, judge all other societies by the same criterion, which results in a disparaging attitude that assumes that highly ritualised societies have everything to learn from us while we have little to learn from them. Nothing could be further from the truth.

This is wrong on two counts: first, while most highly ritualised societies display low levels of technological accomplishment, they are nonetheless highly sophisticated in many other attributes, particularly their social organisation. Highly ritualised societies pay great attention to individual status. To do so is very wise; not to do so is to lay up trouble for the future. Nor should it be forgotten that it is to these very same highly ritualised societies that we are now looking for a solution to one of Western society's longest-standing running sores – the scourge of juvenile delinquency.

Secondly, not all highly ritualised societies are informed by low technology. Japan is the example par excellence of a highly ritualised society of high technology. Japan belies any tacit assumption that the performance and observance of ritual custom is incompatible with economic progress, and although Japan's economy was somewhat in the doldrums during the last decade of the twentieth century, she has not surrendered her position as the world's second largest economy, nor does she look to be in any immediate danger of having to do so.

In highly ritualised societies, adolescents are socialised into young adulthood. These societies provide their adolescents with their exit from one social status and their entrance to the next. For the individual adolescent, for society as a whole, the social benefit of accomplishing this by ordained procedure is incalculable and there is no reason to believe such benefit is not transferable. For this to be so, however, the ordained procedure cannot be blindly copied: Western society must invoke its power of originality and think and devise for itself – a challenge it can easily engage.

THE HOMOGENEITY OF THE SEXES

The phrase 'the homogeneity of the sexes' is designed to convey the idea that, in Western society at least, role differentiation is less determined by sex than ever before. For the most part, roles and occupations are not gender-based. The biological fact of sex used to be a key determinant to social occupation, but this is no longer the case.

In the twentieth century, juvenile delinquency was primarily a male phenomenon and few young offender institutions received juvenile females, but times have changed. Of the 60 young offender institutions in England and Wales, no less than 10 now admit females. A number of female prisons have special wings for juvenile female offenders. The annual publication *Criminal Statistics, England and Wales* shows a year by year rise in the numbers of female offenders. Why is this happening?

Juvenile females are living, working, playing in the same day-to-day world as their juvenile male counterparts. This situation breeds osmosis. Behavioural patterns of the adolescent male are now embracing the female psyche. The phenomenon of 'ladette' behaviour illustrates this. Copy-cat behaviour is not just limited to juveniles. One notices, in this first decade of the twenty-first century, female models tending towards the androgynous. Women are beginning to match men epidemiologically: lung cancer and heart disease were once predominantly male afflictions. Now they are not. How long this will continue is a matter of speculation. Perhaps for not too long. Some women regard 'equal opportunity', the Holy Grail of the Female Liberation movement, as something of a poisoned chalice. They are voluntarily renouncng position and power for the traditional role of housewife and mother.

The sex differential cannot be ignored. Although both sexes experience the onset of puberty – girls a little earlier than boys – the menstrual cycle confirms, and every month re-confirms, the young female in her newly acquired womanhood. The young male has no comparative equivalent and despite the homogeneity of the sexes, the feeling of 'difference' is still in the background. This feeling has been highlighted in response to a particular proposition cited in the survey mentioned above in Chapter 5:

> Males and females, *socially* speaking, mature into adults in *different* ways and by *different* processes? Disagree / Agree

to which 83% of boys and 92% of girls agreed. No other proposition put (in 1995) to the 530 schoolchildren surveyed (335 boys, 195 girls) achieved such a high percentage of likeminded response; in this case, agreement. Of the 104 (all male) young offenders consulted, 87% (90) also agreed with the proposition.

Such a survey is, numerically, indicative – but not conclusive. Attitudes may have radically changed since 1995, but I doubt it. Most women, I believe, have reservations concerning the limits to which they should allow themselves fully to embrace equal opportunity. How many consciously wish to eschew having a family to further a career is surely doubtful. For this reason I propose that as far as possible exit-and-entrance programmes should be delivered on a single-sex basis. The sexes should receive and perform their programmes, for the most part, separately.

There is yet a further reason for advocating an each-sex-on-its-own approach: many highly ritualised societies of low technology all over the world mature their children in an own-sex setting. The implications are considerable. First of all, these societies are, or certainly were, pre-literate. Secondly, they had little or no inter-communication with each other. Thirdly, they have all established their exit-and-entrance programmes to adjust their children's social status seemingly independently. Fourthly, they have predominantly done so in an own-sex setting. They have all, so to speak, independently come to the same conclusion.

A universal human mind seems to be at work. Why contradict it?

12
THEORY OF RITE OF PASSAGE

FROM ONE STATUS TO ANOTHER

I CONSIDER THE FAILURE of Western society to mark the transition from childhood to young adulthood to be a primary cause of juvenile delinquency: the point of failure being that, from the child's point of view, the childhood status lingers on. Seen another way, would-be young adults are rarely, if ever, formally detached from childhood status. There has been no ceremonial cut-off point where childhood ends and young adulthood begins.

Highly ritualised societies mark this transition through two social mechanisms: ritual action and ritual language. The two are not mutually exclusive, but operate together and interactively. Ritual language here refers principally to mode of address. A prescribed mode of address will publicly define personal status – or lack of it. Change in mode of address will signify adjustment and change in personal social status. How much a young person is conscious of his status cannot be over-emphasised. Effectively divorcing himself from childhood is the key social objective. Perverse as it may seem, juvenile delinquency or adolescent misbehaviour is a self-instituted stratagem to induce change in personal status.

Let us first look at ritual action. Most well known is the social mechanism of 'rite of passage' or, in its original French form, *rite de passage*. The word 'passage' refers to 'passage' as in passage from one physical place to another; and then, by extension, from one *social* position to another. The dictionary definition of the word 'rite' defines it as 'a religious or solemn observance or act'. Rite, in the term 'rite of passage', is 'that religious or solemn observance or act' by which (social) 'passage' is achieved.

The word 'rite' should not be confused with its homonym 'right', defined, in one of its many definitions, as 'a thing one may legally or morally claim'. There is no *'right'* of passage; nor any 'right' to rite of passage!

LES RITES DE PASSAGES

Belgian anthropologist Arnold van Gennep's *Les Rites de Passages* was published in 1909. Before discussing his thoughts and observations, one initial point must be made: nearly a century ago, highly ritualised societies were regarded with less respect than they are now. Terms such as 'savage' and 'semi-civilised' were bandied around without a second thought. Technological prowess was automatically associated with greater 'civilisation' and the process of understanding highly ritualised societies was only just beginning. We must therefore be indulgent of descriptions that are now not only politically incorrect but fundamentally wrong.

Van Gennep interested himself in the rituals of highly ritualised societies of low technology, their role and purpose. The definition of ritual, its separation from entertainment theatre, and, above all, its unique power to effect change of social status has been addressed above in Chapter 9. Van Gennep classified rituals according to type. He also classified the various life stages where he found ritual taking place: pregnancy and childbirth, birth and childhood, initiation rites, betrothal and marriage, funeral rites, and so on.

There were other occasions too: passage from one territory to another was never just a simple matter of showing a passport. It was a highly dangerous move in which gods and spirits had to be propitiated. In highly ritualised societies, the act of separation, departure from current status, is anything but casual. It's very often regarded as a form of spiritual 'death'; an essential pre-requisite for the programme of metamorphosis to new status. Van Gennep (1977) wrote:

> A society is similar to a house divided into rooms and corridors. The more the society resembles ours in its form of civilisation, the thinner are its internal partitions and the wider and more open are its doors of communication. In a semi-civilised society, on the other hand, sections are carefully isolated, and passage from one to another must be made through formalities and ceremonies. (p. 26)

EXIT – ABSENCE – ENTRANCE

Van Gennep noticed something else: while particular rituals differed in this or that way from culture to culture in matters of content, their form exhibited universal characteristics. Rituals have structure. In simple terms, rituals have a beginning, a middle and end – they're tri-partite. Van Gennep defines the beginning stage as 'separation'; the middle as 'a transitional period with gradual removal of barriers'; the end as 'reintegration into ordinary life'.

In Chapter 3, above, I referred to Shakespeare's exits and entrances in the Seven Ages of Man. There follows from this the idea of seeing the rite of passage as a sandwich: exit and entrance being the outer covers to the rite-of-passage ritual with the middle as the inner filling! A period of absence often defines the middle, or transitional, section of a ritual; or, to use our latest analogy, the filling in the ritual sandwich.

Absence is a very powerful technique. Although in itself of no consequence, if absence endures in a secret location and/or 'secret' information is imparted, or even if absolutely nothing happens at all but something is said to happen, then the all-important ingredient of 'mystique' enters the equation. The length of absence largely depends on the *purpose* of the absence. If it is to give people time to forget, then the longer the better. If it is to secure a private moment of privacy, during which something mystical may be thought to take place, then five or ten minutes may be enough. The formula for this:

> absence ⇨ secrecy ⇨ mystique = background conditions for effecting change of social status

is effective both for 'cast' and 'audience'. Very often, the audience is itself part of the cast. Both parties, cast and audience, find the whole process entirely credible. This is important for successful re-integration into ordinary life, marking the final stage of a rite of passage.

Absence highlights the act of separation that is the first stage of a rite of passage. Many cultures hold that a person 'dies' from the status he or she is trying to leave. Absence renders this instinct more credible; the more so if, as we have said, the location of the absence is kept secret. The idea of death and rebirth is very clear. The transition achieved by rite of passage is so strong that it's possible to conceive of an entirely new persona being born and transfused into a pre-existing and familiar body.

Page (1972), in a rather spoilsport way, has blown the lid on the underlying rationale for a charming custom we all love:

> The absence ritual with which readers will be most familiar is the twentieth-century Western institution of the honeymoon. In the same way that the Akemba (a West African people) pretend that the purpose of teenage retreats in the bush is to ensure that the boys are capable of achieving erection, so we maintain the pleasant fiction that a honeymoon's function is to enable the groom and bride to embark on their love life together in the most romantic circumstances available.
>
> In reality, of course, the main reason many couples go away is because they feel it is expected of them: and it is expected of them because relatives and friends need a breathing space

> mentally to readjust to the idea that they are now husband and wife, which the wedding ceremony itself is too abrupt to provide. (p. 67)

A honeymoon destination is often kept secret. Secrecy aids mystique. When Sue Jones marries John Smith and returns home as *Mrs* Sue Smith (in British tradition, at least), something mystical can be believed to have happened to her to have aided the transformation.

Page (1972, p. 65) defines an absence ritual as 'an act of temporary withdrawal from the tribal community for a reason other than the stated one'.

ABSENCE MAKES THE HEART GROW FONDER

Absence ritual is a powerful transformational tool. Page (1972) has noted its use in the political arena. In 1969 Paul Hasluck, he recalls, was appointed Governor-General of Australia. The role calls for total impartiality and Hasluck was anything but impartial. Until his appointment he had been, according to Page, Australia's acerbic and controversially hard-line Minister of External Affairs.

How did Hasluck make the transition? He flew to London, saw the Queen, and received her ritual blessing. He returned to Australia. He did *not* move into the Governor-General's residence. Instead, he betook himself to a remote desert farmhouse. He became totally incommunicado. After a good few months, he emerged, ritually reborn, and progressed regally to Canberra. No political fuss, no outcry, no memories of previous partiality; lo and behold one brand new Governor-General in perfect working order! Hasluck, or his advisers, had devised a perfect rite-of-passage; whether consciously, or not, is unknown.

Initiation ceremonies are of all sorts: enthronement of a king or queen; ordination of priests; induction into Freemasonry; admission of apprentices into crafts; and so on. Many of them incorporate, consciously or unconsciously, this technique of prior ritual absence. This even extends to popular entertainment, through the notion of an artist's comeback: to revitalise their career, and often to change creative direction, a performer may disappear from public view (absence), to re-emerge 'reborn' in a new guise. A notable example of this was Bob Dylan's apparent death in the mid-1960s after a motorcycle crash. When he returned to the public arena after a suitable interval, he looked and sounded startlingly different, but his absence (like that of a honeymoon) allowed his millions of fans 'a breathing space mentally to readjust to the idea' of his transformation.

PHYSICAL VS SOCIAL PUBERTY

In discussing the transformation of minors into adults, van Gennep (1977, p. 65) made an important observation: he found it necessary to distinguish between physiological puberty and what he called social puberty. Moreover, the two, he said, rarely, if ever, coincide. Physical puberty occurs when it does, variably between the ages of 12 and 16. Social puberty in contrast occurs whenever a particular culture *ordains* that it does. This varies from culture to culture; and within a culture, it may vary from individual to individual. This in turn will depend on whether an individual has fulfilled whatever social obligations are imposed upon on him or her. La Fontaine (1985) writes:

> Among the Gisu of Uganda, where I did my field-work in the 1950s, no man, however old he might be, was considered adult, and therefore entitled to drink beer on equal terms with other men, unless he were initiated. An uninitiated man, even married and a father, would be referred to contemptuously as a boy. (p. 103)

Similarly, she adds, among another African people, the Bemba, maturity rituals were essential for girls to become real women: 'uninitiated girls were "rubbish"'. La Fontaine (1985) continues:

> These cases are examples of the general fact that among those peoples who perform rituals at maturity, the identity of initiates is a matter of public knowledge and concern, not a secret. Those individuals who escape initiation are known and, usually despised. (ibid.)

Having considered rites of passage in theory, in the next part I will examine in more detail how the passage into adulthood is managed in practice in two very different cultures, the low technology society of the Maassai and the high-technology society of Japan.

Part IV

The Maasai Way

The Maasai Warrior

'to become a warrior is the dream of every Maasai youth: the world seems to convey magical powers. A warrior must be strong, clever, courageous, confident, wise and gentle.[....] In addition to the practical services they provide for the group they live among, warriors also add an immeasurable sense of excitement, adventure and romance; without their songs, their poetry, their flirting, their bold masculinity, Maasai life would not be the same' (Tepilit Ole Saitoti 1980, p. 124). **How far we are from being able to praise our own youth in these terms!**

© Ariadne van Zandbergen / AfriPics.com

13
The Two Models

Maasai and Japanese

In this section of the book, the child-to-adult programmes of two very different societies are reviewed: both are highly ritualised societies – one, of low technology, the Maasai; the other, of high technology, the Japanese. The two societies are very different from each other and the ways in which they manage their child-to-adult exit-and-entrance processes are equivalently different. How other people manage their affairs helps us manage ours. We are afforded the opportunity to be eclectic; we are able to select, to pick and choose in form and content.

According to Wikipedia:

> The Maasai are an indigenous African ethnic group of semi-nomadic people located in Kenya and northern Tanzania. Due to their distinctive customs and dress and residence near the many game parks of East Africa, they are among the most well-known African ethnic groups internationally. The Maasai maintain many of their cultural traditions while engaging contemporary regional and global economic, social, and political forces. They speak Maa, also known as Kimaasai. In 1994 the Maasai population in Kenya was estimated to be 453,000, and in 1993 the Tanzanian Maasai population was estimated at 430,000, for a total estimated Maasai population of 883,000
>
> http://en.wikipedia.org/wiki/Maasai

Our description of the Maasai child-to-adult initiation process derives from Maasai tradition. The extent to which these traditions are followed these days varies. Maasai people living in urban environments may have lost touch with traditions still maintained by those living in a rural environment.

In all cultures whose mores are far removed from those of Western society, one has to accept that there are no universals. Even a concept such as juvenile delinquency must be culturally determined. Indeed, in our own culture, what is considered acceptable and unacceptable varies from age to age. For example, before the Second World War, the cinema came in for heavy censure. Burt (1938) writes:

> It is in the general and more elusive influences that the real danger of the cinema lies. Throughout the usual picture-palace programme, the moral atmosphere presented is an atmosphere of thoughtless frivolity and fun, relieved only by some sudden storm of passion with occasional splashes of sentiment. Deceit, flirtation, and jealousy, unscrupulous intrigue and reckless assault, a round of unceasing excitement and the extremes of wild emotionalism, are depicted as the normal characteristics of the everyday conduct of adults. The child, with no background to correct the picture, frames a notion, altogether distorted, of social life and manners. [...] Far better is it that notions and images of vice should never be placed before his eyes at all. (pp. 148–9)

In today's environment, if visiting the cinema were thought to be a palliative for adolescent misbehaviour, society would settle for it without a second thought. Burt, was writing in 1938, a dozen or so years before the general advent of television in the home in the early 1950s. Television was to provide even greater access to knowledge of the evils of life than cinema. Presumably, television supplanted cinema as the new *bête noire* motivating delinquency – a stigma from which it has yet to recover. For the sake of fairness and balance, Burt (1938) was prepared to admit:

> I could, I think, cite more than one credible instance where the opening of a picture-palace had reduced hooliganism among boys, withdrawn young men from the public-house, and supplied the girls with a safer substitute for lounging with their friends in the alleys or the parks. (p. 150)

Whatever the differences between Western culture today and its pre-war equivalent, the situation of Japan is certainly different. Criteria for juvenile misbehaviour in Japan may differ from criteria used in the West, but knocking an old lady on the head and stealing her handbag is a crime in any culture. With this in mind, it's worth noting that in Japan, in 1993, just 353 Japanese young offenders under the age of 20 were put into custody (Yokoyama, 1996), while in England and Wales the equivalent figure was 13,200 (Home Office, 1997). Japan's population is double Britain's at over 120 million, which makes the Japanese figure even more remarkable.

As for the Maasai, while statistics are lacking there are reasons to believe in its success: one doesn't hear Maasai complain of 'immature youth' – not, at least, in rural environments where traditional culture still obtains. Maasai speak in great praise of their matured and initiated youth and the role they perform for Maasai society.

The Maasai and Japanese have developed, until very recent times, completely unaware of each other's existence and might be surprised to think they had anything in common with each other. In technological terms these societies are poles apart, but in important aspects they are not. They both have 'a scheme of things' for moving the members of their society from one social position to another – an exit-and-entrance programme – and we must follow suit.

14
Maasai Rite of Passage

This account of rite-of-passage procedures among the Maasai derives from Tepilit Ole Saitoti's book on his people (Saitoti, 1980). The Maasai are a warrior people. As cattle herders, they will do almost anything to increase their cattle herd, including raiding neighbours' herds, Maasai and non-Maasai.

It is in this environment that children grow up. In Maasai villages, boys of three or four are often to be seen holding a stick, which symbolises future life as a cattle herder. As a boy gets older, he acquires a taller and pointed stick, which represents a warrior's spear. From the age of seven or eight, the boy has his eye on his future as a warrior. Frequent injuries result from fights with these spear-like sticks. It's all preparation for the future.

On the language side, Maasai children are taught to be respectful; all elders are called 'father', and all women 'mother'. One notes the use of ritual language, ritual mode of address.

Seven to nine year olds start to play at night. A favourite game is pretending that a lion has attacked the herd. The youngsters go charging off pretending they're warriors in pursuit. The game is, one supposes, a Maasai equivalent to cowboys and Indians. Between nine and twelve, games get rougher and tougher. They're played at night under a bright moon. On dark nights, both boys and girls go indoors to listen to the stories and legends of the old days. All storytelling takes place at night. To tell stories during the day would be to risk the loss of cattle – an unthinkable catastrophe.

Towards initiation

The imperative towards adulthood is overwhelming. Boys and girls apparently spend hours checking whether, and to what extent, their pubic hair has grown. Boys, particularly, are given (and give themselves) a hard time: they fight; they're beaten; and when they're beaten by warriors, they must 'take it' without retaliating. Their lack of status, as uncircumcised boys, is accentuated in every way. Uncircumcised youths are made to wear plain togas (Maasai dress is said to derive from Roman times). They're not allowed to wear ornaments or carry a warrior's spear. They're not allowed to congregate and are often beaten if they do. They cannot shake hands with other men as equals; they must continue to bend their heads in the respectful greeting of a child. The whole thing is the more unjust for, as often as not, youngsters, by the ages of 14–16, are performing warrior roles of cattle herding and cattle protection.

There is in this injustice a certain psychology. Injustice intensifies desire for promotion to full warrior status. Promotion however is not automatic. There is no 18th birthday as in Western society, when adult, or in Maasai terms, warrior, status is automatically conferred. Even if boys are of appropriate age, they may still have to wait a long time. Initiation of Maasai youth does not automatically take place when a boy or a girl reaches a particular age. Initiation takes place in a window of time opened and closed by Maasai elders assembled together in conference. The decision to begin (and close) a circumcision period is twofold: first, whether a new set of elders is needed; secondly, whether there's a large enough body of youth waiting in the wings ready to take over. Once decided upon, a circumcision period will last three to four years. When closed, however, there may not be another one for as much as another 15 years.

Meanwhile boys start to show off would-be warrior prowess. They engage in the hunting of particularly dangerous wild animals: lion, buffalo and rhinoceros. By doing so they demonstrate to one and all their strength and ability to protect and defend Maasailand. Yet they still can't become warriors; not until they're circumcised.

We see here the validity of van Gennep's distinction between physical and social puberty. These young men will only become warriors when Maasai society ordains that they will; not before.

THE RITUAL OF CIRCUMCISION

When a new circumcision period opens, separation occurs for the band of candidates selected for initiation. This may be regarded as the first stage of van Gennep's three-step rite of passage. Each boy selects a Maasai priest from his father's generation. The priest gives the boy a new 'generation name'; in effect he completely renames him. The now despised status of child/youth can at last be discarded. Each boy will also select a junior elder to act as his sponsor at his circumcision.

In anticipation of circumcision and warrior status that follows, boys are for the first time publicly allowed to congregate. They adopt warrior manners. Councils are held under the guidance of elders. They debate among themselves acceptable norms of behaviour for impending warriorhood. They camp out at night usually near running water. They're allowed to dress in warrior garb: ochred hair and ostrich feather head-dresses. They sing and dance.

This is the intermediate, the transitional period of the rite of passage. It's not the case that all Maasai boys spend an equal amount of time in this intermediary state. Those who just missed circumcision when the last circumcision period closed will be the first to be circumcised when the next three or four year circumcision period opens. In any event, a particular circumcision date is announced two months in advance. This allows essential preparations to be made. These include building a special circumcision hut where boys will recuperate; and preparing honey-beer to be ceremonially consumed by the elders three days before circumcision.

CIRCUMCISION: THE LEAD-UP

Two days before circumcision, the candidate's head is shaved. In preparation for manhood, all childhood belongings are given away; not a single item may be kept. Interestingly and by way of parallel, those entering Catholic Holy Orders face similar divestment.

The day before circumcision, the Maasai boy meets his circumcisers. They are not Maasai. For whatever reason, circumcision is always performed by non-Maasai. The operation is performed by members of another tribe, the Ndorobo. The circumcisers will, however, give the boy the specially made circumcision knife to be used; it's the boy's job to sharpen it; to keep it overnight; to make sure it doesn't fall into the hands of anyone wishing him harm. This is not as far-fetched as it sounds. Maasai folklore abounds with such stories.

A lot depends on a boy's bearing during circumcision. Not only his, but his family's, reputation is as stake. The objective is to withstand the agony of circumcision without flinching, without literally moving a muscle. There's no anaesthetic; only axe-water, water kept out overnight with a steel axe-head in it to keep it (anaesthetically) cold.

During the day and night before circumcision, crude songs are sung to the boy. These are designed to bolster his courage by angering him:

> Coward, the gray, colorless birds will be yours.
>
> Brave man, the red-winged touracos will be yours;
>
> and so will the green lovebirds
>
> (Saitoti, 1980, p. 80)

Should the boy cry out in pain or, as the Maasai say, 'kick the knife', shame will descend upon him and his family. Attendance at the pre-prepared family circumcision feast will be shunned. The boy will be allowed to make a headdress, but as the quotation from the song above suggests, only from grey colourless birds. His headdress will be a badge of shame. However this 'mark of Cain' is only temporary; his performance is quickly forgotten and buried in obscurity as Maasai life proceeds apace.

CIRCUMCISION: 'WAKE UP YOU ARE NOW A MAN'

The circumcision ceremony is dramatic. It's a men-only affair (clitoridectomy is similarly women-only). The boy is led out, sits down, and assumes the prescribed position. His sponsoring elder holds his back. The call is made: 'one cut'. Circumcision is carried out; the boy's demeanour is carefully monitored. Tension is relieved when the circumciser calls out for milk to wash the boy and the blood from the knife. There are cries of praise and the boy is addressed with the ritual words: '*Wake up, you are now a man.*'

The final part of a Maasai youth's rite of passage is his reintegration into Maasai life. This will be a gradual process. During the three to four years a circumcision period is open, boys will travel the length and breadth of Maasailand visiting compounds where circumcisions are taking place. During these peregrinations, boys are fed especially well. Some will be awaiting circumcision, others recovering from it; for both conditions Maasai feel the need to build their boys up. Life therefore before and immediately after circumcision is an endless series of parties.

Reality returns when a circumcision period closes. As mentioned, it may be as long as 15 full years before another opens. You might think that if you couldn't get circumcision in one part of Maasailand, you could get it in another, but this isn't so. Initiation is totally co-ordinated throughout the whole of Maasailand. It has been so from time immemorial.

For girls, it's different. Playing children's games with boys stops at physical puberty. Uncircumcised adolescent girls are dated and feted by warriors. During the day, girls learn homecraft: cooking, sewing, cleaning, and childcare. Girls are 'circumcised' (clitoridectomy) around the age of 16. Unlike boys, girls are not in age sets. Decision when to circumcise is a family one. Circumcision for girls heralds marriage to a junior elder who will be between the age of 26 to 35, ten or even twenty years older than she is. Circumcision marks the end of a period of free sexual abandon with warriors.

15
Interesting Parallels

The judge and the little boy

It's time to pause and consider – to observe the importance of the interval and the absence. So in this chapter and the next I would like to make a few observations, directly or indirectly related to the initiation rites of the Maasai and how we may be able to apply it to our Western culture.

A few years ago I attended a conference at a young offenders institution called Glen Parva in the English county of Leicestershire. A judge who was present referred to an eight-year-old boy who had appeared before him the previous week for bad behaviour of some sort. The judge told the little boy that he was about to visit this place called Glen Parva. The judge was trying to frighten the little boy: he told him that if his behaviour didn't improve, he might end up locked up in Glen Parva. The boy's face suddenly lit up: 'But that's the name of the place I want to get into as soon as I get to the right age.'

The judge confessed himself surprised and depressed.

The Maasai child is growing up within a 'scheme of things'. The English child is not. Even at this early age, the English boy is clearly under the influence of anti-Establishment forces. As it happens, the norms of Maasai children and this particular English child are not that far apart. The two little children have more in common than might at first be thought. The English judge would be just as taken aback were a Maasai child to declare to him, as he almost certainly would: 'I want to raid (for which understand 'steal') as many cattle as I can as soon as I'm old enough!'

However, the values of these two cultures are not mutually inter-changeable!

Surly behaviour: expected, tolerated, admired

There seems to be an interesting parallel between youth in highly ritualised society and in Western society: in all cases they go through a period of appallingly bad behaviour. This ranges from 'angry young man' syndrome to outright criminality. The angry young man, as many readers will know from their own experience, will fly off the handle at any enquiry beyond a first 'How are you?'

Amazingly, in highly ritualised societies, Maasai included, such delinquency is (a) expected, (b) tolerated and (c) in many cases, admired! The attitude towards juvenile delinquency in less ritualised Western society couldn't be more different: it isn't tolerated, it's not expected and it's definitely not admired!

Van Gennep (1977) was among the first to notice the phenomenon and perhaps the first to explain why:

> During the novitiate, the young people can steal and pillage at will or feed and adorn themselves at the expense of the community. (p. 114)

Brain (1979) writing on Australian aboriginal youth talks of:

> the unbridled independence and unruly temper of the uninitiated boy. (p. 178)

La Fontaine (1985), working among the Gisu people of Uganda, writes of the many times

> I was told that no one could sue a novice for damage done to crops or other possessions, or even take offence at anything said. I was also told of an initiand who hit his father's brother, an unthinkable act in normal circumstances, but the older man ignored it. (p. 139, n. 11)

La Fontaine describes the violent emotion that Gisu call *litima*. This is, she says, violent emotion characteristic of Gisu men:

> It is the origin of quarrels and the cause of violence; but it is also the basis for the independence and competitiveness that Gisu admire in men, and in this context it is the source of eagerness to undergo initiation. The recognized end of the preparatory activities is that the initiands should be in a state of high emotion. The combination of continuous exercise, better-than-normal food, lack of sleep, and general excitement, induces a condition in the novices which resembles a state of trance or disassociation; they speak in a special yodel and appear not to understand what is said to them. Older 'brothers', already initiated, accompany them, protecting bystanders from their wild behaviour and the novices from blundering into things. Gisu see this as evidence of a single-minded violent drive to be initiated, but they also describe the novices as wild, and the novices are not held accountable for things they may do in this state. To the observer they appear

> to be giving an impression of untamed humanity, outside normal society; they are powerful but asocial. (p. 122)

'Untamed humanity', 'outside normal society', 'powerful but asocial': don't these words also describe the 'angry young men' that go to make up our juvenile delinquents and our young offenders? Don't they also describe the behaviour of youngsters whose behaviour is rude, fractious and antisocial, but within (sometimes only just within) the law?

Is there not in the way in which an avuncular and well-meaning judiciary almost falls over backwards not to convict youngsters, not to lock them up, an unconscious realisation that their delinquency, vicious as it often is, is nevertheless motivated by a condition that has descended upon them?

SVENGALI-EFFECT: PUPPETS ON A STRING

Such perception, if it is there, is well founded. Youngsters the world over, young males especially, are overtaken by a mindset that, Svengali-like, descends upon them. They are puppets on a string, victims of a force which they don't know exists and consequently over which they have no control. This force has a sociological name: it's called 'social fact'. The term was invented in 1895 by the French sociologist Durkheim (1982). He defined a social fact as:

> any way of acting, whether fixed or not, capable of exerting over the individual an external constraint (p. 59)

Social facts are very powerful. Durkheim continues:

> far from their being a product of our will, they determine it (our will) from without. They are like moulds into which we are forced to cast our actions. (p. 70)

And again on the 'social fact':

> the individual finds himself in the presence of a force which dominates him and to which he must bow. But this force is a natural one. It is not derived from some conventional arrangement which the human will has contrived, adding it on to what is real; it springs from the heart of reality itself; it is the necessary product of given causes. (p. 143)

If all this is going on in the background, it's not difficult to present a case that more or less exonerates young people from the consequences of their misdemeanours. Low-technology highly ritualised societies appear to do just that. However, it should be stressed that they don't allow their patience in this regard to be tried for too long; tolerance lasts a comparatively short time during the build-up and aftermath of initiation. This tolerance, acceptance and, above all, understanding of Angry Young Man syndrome suggests that highly ritualised low-technology societies are more attuned to the vagaries of the human condition than their Western counterparts. A sobering thought! Highly ritualised societies realise that the imperative working upon adolescents, namely, the vital need to make the adjustment in social status from child to young adult, is one that must be engaged; it's an imperative moreover which 'springs from the heart of reality itself' (Durkheim, 1982, p. 143, quoted above).

From an adolescent Maasai's point of view, and indeed, from the point of view of any other adolescent in any other human culture, the force at work upon him will be beyond his individual ability to control it. In many ways this impetus for change in personal status is comparable to the sex drive; but, like the sex drive it will vary in intensity from individual to individual. For van Gennep (1977) there was no problem. He divined immediately why young people's delinquency is ignored in highly ritualised societies. He realised that in the rite-of-passage process you have to go outside society before you can come back into it:

> The novices are outside society, and society has no power over them, especially since they are sacred and holy, and therefore untouchable and dangerous, just as gods would be. Thus........the society is defenseless against the novices' undertakings. That is the explanation – the simplest in the world – for a fact [young people stealing and pillaging whilst awaiting initiation] that has been noted among a great many peoples and that has remained incomprehensible to observers. (p. 114)

For a relatively short period, youngsters in highly ritualised societies are outlaws. No one is more desirous than they themselves to re-enter society as fully fledged young members of the establishment. Their time as outlaws is short. In contrast, many Western youth spend many years out in the cold. They will reach the age of 30 or 35 before they start to settle down. Only middle age will finally quell the inexplicable internal anger. Only then will anger and confusion slowly transform into maturity.

The point is worth re-iterating: in highly ritualised societies juvenile delinquency is expected, tolerated and admired. Because everyone knows, actors (i.e. angry young men) and audience alike, that the Angry Young Man syndrome is not going to last all that long. In the scheme of things, as the ritual drama progresses, the juvenile will soon be re-integrated into the establishment.

DEATH AND DESTINY

Saitoti (1980) portrays the status of Maasai warriorhood in lyrical terms:

> to become a warrior is the dream of every Maasai youth; the world itself seems to convey magical powers. A warrior must be strong, clever, courageous, confident, wise and gentle. He must hunt lions for his headdress, protect his herds from predators, retrieve stolen or strayed cattle, often from long distances, and safeguard his community [...] In addition to the practical services they provide for the group they live among, warriors also add an immeasurable sense of excitement, adventure and romance; without their songs, their poetry, their flirting, their bold masculinity, Maasai life would not be the same. (p. 124)

This desire to become a warrior may indeed be the dream of every Maasai youth. But one wonders why. The Maasai initiation process is truly destiny-testing. Not every Maasai youth survives: a very small number succumb to circumcision wounds: not just Maasai, but young men from all highly ritualised societies of low technology that traditionally practise scarification and, in particular, circumcision. No accurate statistics are available but the figure is unlikely to be higher than 2% and probably nearer 1%.

La Fontaine (1985, pp. 98, 114) tells of death in initiation among the Mende people in West Africa and of two boys who died from their wounds during her own fieldwork among the Gisu in 1954. Circumcision and scarification is conducted without anaesthetic and without properly sterilised implements. Antibiotics are often unavailable to treat subsequent infection.

Public reaction to death in initiation is interesting. La Fontaine (1985, p. 98) relates the ritual formula used by the Mende. An elder declares to the parents: 'I am sorry to tell you that the pot you have given me to fire is broken.' La Fontaine says that whatever private feelings a family may have a boy who dies in initiation is treated as if he had never existed. The Xhosa in South Africa go further. They believe that those who don't survive initiation are those that aren't destined by the spirits to reach manhood. The belief still persists.

In highly ritualised societies, death in initiation is not an occasion for a 'lawyers' banquet'. It's not treated as an outrageous breach of Health and Safety regulations. No one threatens to sue. The child is publicly forgotten. His death signifies that, for whatever reason, he was never destined by the spirits to reach manhood. That's all there is to it.

Belief that achieving manhood, or not achieving manhood, is a matter of destiny is not just confined to highly ritualised societies. It seems to pre-occupy youth in Western societies. They too challenge destiny and actively court death in the process.

In Chapter 6, above, joyriding and drug-taking were presented as examples of Western youth's challenge to destiny. Joyriding was labelled 'destiny-testing', as was drug-taking in its initial pre-addictive stage.

Destiny, the spirits, fate – these are all names for the same goddess. We shall simply call her Destiny: the goddess who dwells at the very back of every human mind. She looms into the consciousness of her subjects from time to time, such as during transition, official transition or self-attempted transition. Once the decision has been taken to exit the childhood life stage, travel is compulsory along whatever dangerous passage connects to the next life stage. It is here, somewhere in this dangerous corridor, that our goddess lurks and reigns supreme. She, and she alone, will capriciously ordain success or failure for all who attempt to make the perilous journey. She is in control moreover, wherever the journey is made, be it in the delirium of those who succumb to the unsterilised knife; or those who insanely career round the streets of London, Rome or New York, or the drug-taker who lives and dies in his or her overdose.

Destiny holds sway over Maasai and Western youth alike. She seems to find it utterly irrelevant whether transition from childhood to young adulthood is socially managed, as it is with the Maasai, or whether it isn't, as with their Western counterparts. In both environments, there are those that 'don't make it', those whom Destiny has tested and whom she has capriciously decided to fail.

Highly ritualised low technology societies regard their initiation procedures as private and sacred. This attitude is understandable and commands respect. With this caveat in place, it is possible to speculate that pro rata, death and permanent injury are greater from joy-riding, drug-taking and the many other forms of Western destiny-testing than they are from misadventure in tribal initiation.

16
Masonic and Jewish Initiation Rites

Initiation into Freemasonry: A Western Rite of Passage

In Chapter 10 (above), Freemasonry was advanced as an example of how members of Western societies are, when it suits them, quite capable of immersing themselves in ritual behaviour. Initiation into Freemasonry reveals a classic three-stage rite of passage. The three stages are: exit or separation from existing status; actually dangerous, or ritually dangerous, adventure along a path or corridor of transformation; and entrance to the next status.

There are two reasons for describing the ceremony: first, discounting the fact that much of our everyday behaviour is bizarre to an outsider – we can't see the wood for the trees – initiation into Freemasonry is bizarre by our own standards. This highlights the overall point: namely, Western man's ability to perform ritual is just as great as anybody else's. Secondly, from an eclectic point of view, when creating a domestic programme, the more practices one can extrapolate from close to home, the better.

Initiation into Freemasonry usually takes place in one session. The candidate may have had to spend time learning in advance ritual passages and responses. Knight (1983) gives a comprehensive description of Masonic initiation. This brief outline is taken from his work.

The first part of the rite, in van Gennep terms, is the rite of separation. In the case of the initiate Freemason, he is being separated from his life as hitherto led. He is portrayed as 'a poor Candidate in a state of darkness' (p. 313). This condition is constructed with a high degree of drama and theatricality and in this sense, the rite is no different in form to that of a highly ritualised society. In content it is different, but only insofar as reality is substituted by symbolism.

The rite begins outside the Freemasons' Lodge. The Lodge may be a dedicated Masonic Temple; or it may be any room anywhere temporarily dedicated to Masonic use. Outside the door of the Lodge, whilst Masons are in session, is the Tyler. The Tyler stands outside the Lodge door, dagger in hand. This gentleman is the first line of symbolic defence against non-Masons attempting to enter the Lodge and breach its secrecy.

THE TYLER PREPARES THE CANDIDATE

This is simply done. The candidate is reduced to a dishevelled state; to a poor pathetic disorientated and vulnerable human being, 'a poor Candidate in a state of darkness'. All metal objects are taken away (metal objects – watches, rings and so on – may be presumed to be signs of wealth); outer clothing is removed; the candidate is left in his socks with one shoe on his right foot and a slipper on his left. His left trouser leg is rolled up above the knee. His shirt is unbuttoned and pulled back to reveal a bare left breast; the right sleeve is rolled up above the elbow.

HANGMAN'S NOOSE AND BLINDFOLD

Then a hangman's noose is put on his neck and he's blindfolded. The candidate is introduced to the members of the Lodge. The Inner Guard, another Officer of the Lodge, receives him. The Inner Guard points a dagger to the candidate's left breast.

The candidate can now be said to be in the marginal or middle state of his rite of passage. He is led blindfolded around the four corners of the Lodge in a state of total disorientation. As he's pulled here and there, he relies on his about-to-be fellow Masons not to allow him to stumble. The physical support given also has a metaphorical symbolic implication. Eventually he appears still blindfolded before the current Chairman of the Lodge, the Worshipful Master. There follows a series of ritual questions and answers. Finally the candidate swears his 'obligations'. The candidate avows finally to abide by the rules of the Freemasonry Craft on penalty (Knight, 1983, p. 317):

> on the violation of any of them, than that of having my throat cut across, my tongue torn out by the root, and buried in the sand of the sea at low water mark, or a cable's length from the shore, where the tide regularly ebbs and flows twice in twenty-four hours, or the more effective punishment of being branded as a wilfully perjured individual, void of all moral worth, and totally unfit to be received into this worshipful Lodge, or any other warranted Lodge or society of men, who prize honour and virtue above the external advantages of rank and fortune. So help me, God, and keep me steadfast

> in this my Great and Solemn Obligation of an Entered Apprentice Freemason.

The blindfold and noose are eventually removed after the candidate has made his Obligations. He is then told that had he not stood his ground in the 'ordeal' and had he tried to bolt, he would have gone forward into the dagger pointed by the Inner Guard to his left breast. Had he gone backwards, the rope attached to the noose would have been grasped, causing strangulation!

SYMBOLIC RISK

The marginal, middle stage is thus characterised, however symbolically, by disorientation, danger and possible death. Interestingly, initiation into freemasonry incorporates risk. But the risk is symbolic, not real. On the other hand, as many will testify from personal experience, appearing and performing in public can be full of anxiety. Candidates for initiation have to contend with the risk of stage fright and fluffing lines. Spotlighted attention, declamation of learnt lines, solo performance to a critical public, these are frequently the alternative to life-threatening rituals. Doubtlessly, there are those who might prefer the agony of physical incision, the Russian roulette of joyriding even, to the terror of stage fright!

In terms of risk (putative rather than actual), Masonic initiation ritual is a social change transition ritual similar to childhood to young adulthood rituals in other parts of the world. This is possibly because Masonic candidates are often quite young; similar in age to those in other societies whose childhood social status is discarded by right of passage initiation.

The third stage is integration or entrance. For Masonic candidates, or *Entered* (my italics) Apprentice Freemasons, as they're called, this takes the form of a formal Masonic dinner. This is itself a ritual in its own right. The newly initiated Freemason will enjoy the congratulations of his new-found fellow members in The Brotherhood. He will be formally welcomed with speeches and presentations.

NOT-SO-PHYSICAL AND NON-PHYSICAL RITE OF PASSAGE

Venues for Masonic rites are not clearings in the forests of darkest Africa, the jungles of Peru or the deserts of Australia; Masonic Lodges and Temples are located in the hustle and bustle of most of the towns and cities of Western societies. Men from highly ritualised low technology societies are therefore not a human species constituting a class of their own; when discarding old, and acquiring new social status there is clear similarity. Mason or Maasai, joyrider or drug-taker – they all travel along a dangerous path: they all court danger, actual or putative.

Universality in the human mind seems to be at work. But it may well be that Maasai and Western culture share a penchant for physicality because they are both fundamentally of a warlike or violent disposition. The Maasai child is after all converted into a Maasai warrior for whom physical danger is an ever-present and immediate possibility. Adolescents in some Western societies may feel the same way. But not all cultures are of a warlike disposition – explicitly at least. Some peoples transform their children into young adults without life-threatening ordeals. Levine (1965) notes that when a young Amhara (Ethiopian Christian) reaches puberty he is refused the celebration of Eucharist. There is nothing life-threatening in this. Nevertheless, a change in social status has been marked. The sacrament is only resumed on celebration of marriage. Withdrawal and re-integration, as per van Gennep, is thus achieved in an entirely different way.

Barmitzvah

Jews, in common with Amhara Ethiopian Christians, experience the physicality of circumcision as babes in arms no more than eight days old. Child / young adult ceremonies involve no further physicality. Jewish *barmitzvah* is entirely cerebral. Barmitzvah is an act of affirmation, not confirmation, whose celebration is not obligatory. Nonetheless, among orthodox Jews, from the pre-pubescent age of just 13, young Jews are separated from childhood status. From this age, they are able to constitute a part of the religious quorum of ten 'adult' males *(minyan)* without which a full orthodox Jewish Service cannot take place.

How effective barmitzvah is as a rite of passage is hard to say. It probably depends on the extent to which each individual Jewish boy lives his life within the religious fold. Many Jews are secular and although they have celebrated their barmitzvah, possibly at their parents' behest, the primary focus of their daily lives may be outside the religious arena. Consequently, secular influences, positive and negative, may pre-dominate over religious ones.

But being barmitzvahed has its uses. Blumenkrantz (1996) writes:

> Once, I was introduced to a well known anthropologist, who after hearing my name said, 'You're that psychologist guy who does rites of passage. What gives you the right to work with rites of passage? That's part of anthropology!' Getting past the initial abruptness of this 'scholarly greeting' I responded, 'Well, I was Bar Mitzvahed, you know.' (p. 23)

Barmitzvah for Blumenkrantz was not just a religious convenience; it was a deeply meaningful and symbolic experience. Blumenkrantz relates how he received the honour of parading a *Sefer Torah* (Scroll of the Law) two weeks after his barmitzvah. Looking towards the whole assembled congregation he relates how: 'For the first time, I realize that *I am someone among them.*' He also tells how his newly acquired adult status dawned upon him when his mother received a phone call from his synagogue asking her to send him round to the evening prayers of mourning (*shiva*) for a neighbour who had just died:

> 'Why do I have to go? I didn't even know him,' I declared.
>
> 'Because it is your responsibility as an adult member of the congregation,' my mother told me. 'You don't have to know someone to be included in a *minyan* [the quorum of ten adult males, mentioned above] and sit *shiva,*' she firmly concluded.
>
> I knew that my fate was sealed. (pp. 48–9)

In all societies where there is 'a scheme of things'; where thought has been given to the question of turning children into adults, as Blumenkrantz (1996, pp. 121–89) notes: 'something happened'. In Western society nothing happens – unless, of course, you, or your friends in the gang, organise it yourself.

Part V

The Japanese Way

Knowing your Social Status

Two Japanese business men present their cards in the prescribed way and carefully assess each other's status in the process. He who perceives himself to have the higher status will emerge from the bow first.

Photography: Fstop

17
Rite of Passage vs No Rite of Passage

The Maasai, as we have seen, submit their children to a definable rite of passage. Many other highly ritualised cultures of low technology do the same, but I have selected the Maasai because their culture has been comprehensively described. Intimate details of Maasai culture are thus easy to access. It is also particularly gratifying when a culture is described from the 'inside' by one of its own; in this respect, the work of Saitoti (1980) has been invaluable.

Traditional Maasai culture imposes life-threatening risk on all its male youth; in contrast, Western youth impose upon themselves life-threatening risk. For Western youth, life-threatening risk would include socially acceptable behaviour. This has produced the argument, set out above, that Western youth is at one with youth in highly ritualised societies in the physically dangerous way, potential or actual, by which new or changed social status is acquired.

One could be forgiven for concluding that status change can only be achieved in an atmosphere of life-threatening risk. However, this is not the case, as can be demonstrated by an analysis of the position in Japan. In Japanese society, children have been traditionally transformed into adults without the trauma that characterises the experience of Western society; or without a rite-of-passage process similar to other highly ritualised societies. There is, in Japan, nothing that approximates to the social mechanism of a formal rite of passage. There is no identifiable procedure specifically dedicated to maturing adolescents into young adults.

Japan is unquestionably a highly ritualised society. You can't leave a major Tokyo department store without staff employed purely for the purpose of bowing deeply to you and thanking you for your custom. To complete the mystery: during the last five decades of the twentieth century, Japanese crime rates actually fell while Western crime rates rocketed (Fenwick, 2000; see Appendix 2).

All this cries for an explanation yet none has so far been produced. Western academics and criminologists are aware of Japan's low crime figures: if they could have been replicated in Western societies, they would have been. Every Western government would wish to notch up a success in crime reduction and particularly juvenile delinquency.

The Japanese language

The secret of Japan's success lies in its language, which must be considered within the overall framework of the basic theory put forward at the outset of this study, which was that juvenile delinquency is primarily motivated by the desire to shed existing social status, to achieve exit from childhood and, as soon as possible thereafter, to acquire new social status, to knock on the door marked entrance to adulthood and be accepted into it. In Western culture this has proved a problem. The rules for effecting this transition have never been made explicit to adolescents because, to date, the only rule has been: each man for himself. Rules are made up on the hoof by adolescents themselves. Results are more often than not disastrous. The key question, in the adolescent years, that of precise social status, is answered in the worst possible way – with a nebulous uncertainty. This is the problem.

But what happens when this isn't a problem, if rules are very certain and you have to define the social status of whomever you're talking to in every sentence? And when, in his or her reply, your social status, the respect due to you, is confirmed? You know your social place. Your social status is explicit to you, your peer group and the generations above and below you? If all this happens, there is nothing to worry about; nothing to prove, and everything to lose if formalities cease to be observed – assuming, that is, in the Japanese case, this is linguistically possible.

The Japanese language inherently imposes this kind of rigorous control upon its speakers. It's impossible not to conform. Did the Japanese create their language or did the language create the Japanese? Which is the chicken and the egg? The question is academic and probably unanswerable. What matters is the actual reality.

18
Knowing your Social Status

The Japanese people are born into a social system that ascribes and defines status and dignity during all stages of life. No special attention, therefore, needs to be given, or has been given, to the adolescent stage as such. The mechanisms for social control are long in place by the time a Japanese child has reached adolescence. Nothing major needs to be done.

Social status is embedded in the language. Status is the keyword: it's the failure to change status smoothly that so agitates Western youth; in particular the adolescent's uncomfortable awareness that, status-wise, he might not be accorded the respect he deserves for the change he feels has occurred. So how does language, ritual language, fit into the model that has been constructed?

It's a question of widening the definition of the word 'ritual'. Earlier, ritual was defined as: 'a procedure regularly followed'. The use of the word 'procedure' might imply physical action. But procedure can be extended to include the word 'language' . This properly covers the role ritual language plays in human life. The term 'ritual' thus includes both physical action and verbal utterance, often simultaneously so. A definition for ritual language might state: 'mode or modes of address obligatorily employed'.

Two points follow: physical events such as circumcision, clitoridectomy or scarification are a striking climax to a rite-of-passage process; accompanying and consequential verbal changes in mode of address might be regarded as incidental. After all, there is little effort in changing a mode of address. But the two go together, physical and linguistic. Each is equally important. However in the Japanese model, and this cannot be stressed too highly, an adolescent is effortlessly, unconsciously, turned into a young adult simply by means of evolving patterns in ritual modes of address. There is no physical rite of passage.

A second point is that native speakers of any language are de facto bound by the rules, whatever they may be, for speaking the language. For the most part, people are entirely unconscious of often complicated linguistic rules that govern the language they speak. This applies as much to Japanese as it does to any language: and Japanese people simply cannot avoid employing the rules embedded in the Japanese language for addressing third parties when they are speaking in Japanese. This may seem rather obvious but it needs to be pointed out because, like any language, Japanese embraces all its native speakers by its rules. In the same way any scheme put forward for exiting and entrancing adolescents from one life stage to another must include all young people.

Many programmes have been tried, and many are very worthy. But they all eventually fail for want of including all adolescents in their grip. Anything less will not work. In Japanese culture, the operative mechanism for social control and ritual action is the language of Japanese. The important criterion of every young person being included is thus fulfilled. It is this simple fact alone which accounts for Japan's success in maintaining low figures for youth crime, and crime as a whole.

19
JAPANESE

THE PEOPLE AND THE LANGUAGE

TABOO LANGUAGE

Human beings have instinctively hit upon formal modes of address as a means of establishing social distance. Linguists refer to this as taboo language. Taboo language can include formal modes of address and much besides. The Japanese linguist Takao (1978) writes:

> **Please don't mention the word –'death'!**
>
> In linguistics, a taboo is an act of avoiding a direct reference to a certain object or fact, out of fear of shyness or for religious reasons. When reference to these objects or facts becomes absolutely necessary, they are spoken of indirectly or suggestively by means of other words. (p. 101)

By way of example, among Jews of Spanish origin, a cemetery is referred to as a 'House of Life'. More significantly, reference to people by invoking their occupational, professional or social accomplishments – in other words all reference which avoids use of the personal pronoun 'you', or an individual's personal name – should be called taboo language. (As I will discuss further in the next chapter, Parliamentary modes of address in the Chamber of the House of Commons are a form of 'taboo' language.) All Japanese people, it would appear, want all social interaction all the time to be governed by considerations of deference and hierarchy; taboo language is consequently a uniform feature of Japanese modes of address.

HIERARCHICAL DIFFERENCES AND RESPECT LANGUAGE

Taboo language is the vehicle which conveys politeness and deference, values which are ideals of Japanese culture, about which Hendry (1987) writes:

> There is no doubt that hierarchical differences affect interaction between Japanese people in their everyday lives. Indeed, in many situations it is difficult to know how to behave unless one can place the other people present in a hierarchical order in relation to oneself. This begins from the moment of greeting, for bowing is a good example of the expression of the expression of status differences. One bows more deeply to a superior than to an inferior, and one should stay down longer than one's superior. An amusing situation arises where the relationship is unclear, for each side will try to stay down longer, assuming that it is better to err on the inferior side than on the superior. The custom of exchanging name cards on meeting a new person helps to resolve such problems. (p. 71)

Business cards are presented in Japan in a ritual way in the process of ritual bowing and are held in such a way that the recipient can clearly see the donor's status.

An English business colleague was astonished to see his Japanese business partner receive a telephone call from Japan from an obviously important client and respond by immediately getting up off his chair, standing to attention and bowing deeply – into the phone! This illustrates how deeply ingrained is the hierarchical imperative. There is to it also a language component.

The Japanese have refined the genre of respect language to a sophisticated art. Hendry (1993) discusses this respect language whose Japanese name is keigo. This sub-divides into sonkeigo which raises the level of the person to whom you are speaking, the addressee; then there is kenjogo, or humble language, which lowers the level of the speaker; and finally, teineigo, 'polite language' which raises the general level of speech altogether. As Hendry writes (1993, p. 52):

> These forms of speech are in theory available to all Japanese speakers, and some tuition in their use is given at school. Parents teach their children to speak appropriately to senior members of the family and to teachers, doctors, and other professionals they may encounter together. In the workplace, companies have training courses for their new recruits including instruction in the language they like used with customers. In the kindergarten where I worked in Chiba prefecture, even the teachers were instructed regularly by the head teacher about appropriate forms for the parents of their charges (Hendry, 1986). Nevertheless, manuals about proper usage are available in such abundance in bookshops that it would seem that people still feel they need further guidance. In fact, this language seems to have changed quite

> considerably in the lifetimes of older people in Japan, who regularly lament the lack of correct usage in the modern world. (p. 52)

Hendry's observations are reinforced by the Japanese linguist Takao in his book, *Japanese and the Japanese* (1978). Takao considers Japanese grammar in detail and compares it with European languages. He tells how Japanese linguists, in the late nineteenth century, when compiling the first grammars of Japanese, tried to force their grammars to conform to paradigms long since established by Western grammarians.

He notes how Japanese tables for personal pronouns: 'I', 'thou'/'you', 'he', 'she' etc. do not represent either modern-day or historical linguistic reality. This is especially so for 'I' and 'thou'/'you'. This is understandable in the context of the Japanese cultural imperative to deference behaviour. In this context, Japanese people resort to taboo language which avoids all considerations of 'I' and 'you'. Insofar as these pronouns exist in Japanese, they are employed within the family; in a one-way direction from superior to inferior, i.e. from parent to child or elder to younger sibling.

Inferior to superior relationships within the family are marked by use of descriptive terms: 'father' (*Otosan*), 'older brother' (*Nisan*), 'uncle' (*Ojisan*). Inferior to superior relationships outside the family never involve the use of personal pronouns. The occupational, professional or social status of the person whom you are addressing must be substituted. For example, if you know your teacher's wife has been unwell, and you wish to enquire politely after her health, you must say: 'How is Teacher's wife?' Not 'How is your wife?'

THE LIFE AND EARLY DEATH OF A PRONOUN

Personal pronouns in European languages are not immutable – there is change. For example, the second person singular pronoun 'thou' has fallen into decline in mainstream modern English. Self-reference terms in Japanese, substituting the English first-person singular 'I', however, are very prone to change. They seem to go through some sort of life-cycle. Takao (1978) notes what he calls 'the pattern of vicissitudes of personal pronouns':

> whenever a new pronoun for speaker self-reference comes into use, it first connotes the sense of humility the speaker feels towards the addressee, but as its usage continues, it gradually begins to express the speaker's sense of superiority to the addressee, and finally becomes a word which can be used only when the speaker looks down on the addressee, thus falling out of general use. (p. 99)

Takao concludes:

> The fact that so-called personal pronouns in present-day Japanese are not really words which directly indicate either the speaker or the addressee, but words that indirectly refer to them, as well as the fact that in the history of the language they have frequently replaced one another, definitely shows that they are taboo-related. Indeed, the Japanese have a tendency even today to do without personal pronouns in conversation whenever possible. (p. 101)

I'M YOUR TEACHER – JUST CALL ME 'BOB'

Taboo language, particularly deference in mode of address, is a social device for order and stability in human relations. There are other techniques, though they are perhaps more draconian and less poetic. Taboo language may be found in certain elements of a culture and not in others; or it may permeate throughout. The decision to invoke deference behaviour or taboo language is social. The desire of such a decision is to maintain social distance, to confirm status between superior and inferior and vice versa. After all, in almost all interpersonal relationships, status is present and status is a factor.

Self-reference and mode of address is therefore very revealing. Examining kinship and non-kinship modes of address, and terms for self-reference, is a first focus of enquiry into any culture. All of this is capable of change from decade to decade. Custom changes all the time. When I was at school (1950s), pupils addressed their formmates by their surnames; masters were uniformly 'sir'; first-naming in class was absolute anathema. For the time being there has been a turnaround and familiarity is the current fashion.

Socially prescribed and ritually enforced respect dignifies the individual and reassures him of his social status. Nothing is more important to an adolescent knocking on the door of full adulthood than for his social status to be confirmed. Conversely, nothing is more harmful to an adolescent than for his social status to be blurred and ill-defined. Yet, this is mainly what happens in modern Western society. Here, our whole ethos is directed towards minimisation of social status at the very time when, paradoxically, for young people especially, its clarification is most important. From primary school to university, mutual first-naming has been encouraged in the classroom. Formal teacher–student relationships have largely disappeared.

Everything of course comes at a price. Japanese formality restricts social flexibility within Japanese society in a way which is not the case in Western society. This can be unhealthy as Takao (1978) notes:

> In short, for most Japanese, a relationship between two specific persons is intrinsically a fixed one involving only two roles, e.g., husband and wife, or teacher and student.
>
> A relationship between two Americans, on the other hand, is much more flexible, allowing a far greater variety of roles. This is why husband and wife can be at the same time teacher and student, friends, or even rivals.
>
> When American graduate students earn their doctorates, they soon start calling their former professors by their first names. The reason is that in the United States the concept of colleagueship is an egalitarian one and supersedes differences in seniority. In contrast, I still cannot call an old professor from my university days any term other than Sensei 'Teacher'. This is more than twenty years after graduation. (p. 141)

20
Formal Modes of Address

A Western Parallel

One doesn't necessarily have to go to Japan to see Japanese-type linguistic mores in operation. An analogy is closer to home. The principle at work in Japanese modes of address is to be found in, of all places, the British House of Commons.

Life in the Chamber of the House of Commons is very Japanese-like. Members of Parliament may not be overtly conscious of it, but they are governed by verbal constraints precisely similar to those that mould the daily lives of Japanese speakers. The only difference is that Japanese speakers remain in House of Commons 'mode' *all* the time without any let up.

Speech on the floor of the Chamber is anything but casual. Members' names are sacred. It's the prerogative of the Speaker, and only the Speaker, to use them. And he (or she) does so only on specifically defined occasions, either when calling upon him her to address the House or in 'naming' an MP on a matter of discipline:

> If a member has disregarded the authority of the Chair, or has persistently and wilfully obstructed the House by abusing its rules, he or she (after generally being given every opportunity to set matters to rights) may be named. That is, the Speaker says 'I name Mr. George White' (or whoever). Thereupon, the Leader of the House, the Government Chief Whip, or the senior Minister present, moves 'that Mr. George White be suspended from the service of the House. (House of Commons factsheet No 52, revised April 2000)

In all other situations, use of Members' names is taboo. In the debating Chamber of the House of Commons every Member must be referred to as Honourable – whatever personal feelings there may be. Outside the

Chamber, first (or last) name terms of address may be used, but not inside. The label 'Honourable' used to be further embellished: Honourable and Learned, indicating a legal qualification; Honourable and Gallant, a military background. In recent times, the House of Commons 'Modernisation Committee' has allowed these refinements to fall by the wayside.

MPs are referred to by their constituency: 'the Honourable Member, the Member for Butterfield'; or, they can be referred to as 'the Honourable Gentleman or Honourable Lady'. MPs in your own Party are your Honourable Friends (whether you like them or not). MPs speaking on the floor of the Commons unconsciously follow other conventions of the Japanese language. They must not use the pronoun 'you' (whether as direct or indirect object):

> a Member persistently offending against the tradition, and using 'you' or a Member's name, is likely to be corrected by the Speaker and to be interrupted by shouts of 'order' from other Members. (Factsheet, ibid.)

Thus a simple everyday phrase such as: 'I have to tell you that' will come out as 'I have to tell the Honourable Gentleman that'. Every time you intend to say 'you', the pronoun must be substituted by 'my Honourable friend' or 'the Honourable Gentleman'. On leaving the Chamber, every Honourable Member is obliged to bow to the Speaker. Within the precincts of the Palace of Westminster, Members do not shake hands with each other or, as far as possible, with anybody else.

There are books on Parliamentary language which might as well be manuals on Japanese protocol. How much more Japanese-like can you get? And whoever thought that intense ritualised behaviour is inimical to the British way of life? Surely, these conventions are outmoded – it's amazing they haven't been totally scrapped. It always seems like the obvious thing to do, especially on the inauguration of a new Government.

It was one of the first things Ann Taylor said she had on her list of things-to-do when Prime Minister Tony Blair appointed her Leader of the House on 3 May 1997 (thus elevating her, by the way, to the status of Right Honourable, an accolade accorded to members of the Sovereign's Privy Council). But somehow or other, it never happened. Her programme was quietly dropped. MPs are still to be heard when the House is in session, conferring dignity upon each other in arcane and archaic ritual modes of address.

Why do they continue to do so and why does it matter? Factsheet 52 (cited above) is in no doubt:

> The purpose of this style of address using 'Honourable' is to maintain the dignity of the House and its Members, to make

criticism and comment less direct, and to reduce the asperity of debate, as well as showing respect to the Chair.

PERSONAL PRONOUNS AS SUBJECT AND OBJECT IN DIRECT AND INDIRECT SPEECH

First of all, what is happening linguistically? Linguistically, as noted above, the personal pronoun 'you' has been eliminated from House of Commons parlance (Chamber only) in all forms of direct speech either as subject, object or indirect object. A limited range of honorific titles has been substituted: Honourable Gentleman/Lady etc.

It could be worse: the personal pronoun 'I' is still permitted. For instance, Members can say, 'I must say to the Honourable Gentleman, that so far as I am concerned' and not, for example (and somewhat obsequiously), 'Your Honourable Servant must say to the Honourable Gentleman that so far as Your Honourable Servant is concerned.'

Parliamentary language is not just constrained by a mere restriction on the use of the personal pronoun. The Speaker will immediately upbraid any Member who strays from linguistic parliamentary etiquette: over the centuries, a mass of euphemism, or taboo language as linguists call it, has evolved. Euphemism, taboo language, protects a Member's integrity and safeguards it from gratuitous attack.

There are ways of getting round the system. Linguistic felicities are employed to convey what you mean – especially when you can't say what you mean in direct terms. Some readers may be familiar with Winston Churchill's instant substitution, at the Speaker's intervention, of the word 'lie' (very definitely, not allowed) for 'terminological inexactitude' (apparently permissible).

So on a broader scale, what is happening?

RITUAL 'SUPERSTRUCTURE' – AND REBELLION

First, a substantial superstructure of (linguistic) ritual has been created. Within this ritual superstructure debate takes place. The temperature of debate varies from civilised discussion to furious altercation. The superstructure of linguistic ritual easily enables extreme discord and dissension to be accommodated. Indeed, the layout of the Chamber of the House of Commons is more designed for conflict than consensus. The Chamber has often been compared to a bear garden – described in Brewer's Dictionary of Phrase and Fable as 'a place of tumult and disorder'.

Gluckman (1966) puts forward an interesting proposition: the greater the extent to which a superstructure of ritual is in place, the greater the room for ritual disorder within it. More than this, he concludes, such disorder is very healthy, desirable even; ritual disorder tests, reinforces and substantiates the established order. Ritually turning things on their head is not confined to highly ritualised societies: Gluckman noted for example (p. 109) that in certain armed services at Christmas, and at Christmas only, officers wait at table on the men. This is a 'mild' form of role reversal.

Some highly ritualised societies go much further than this: ritual 'rebellions' which appear to go within an ace of overthrowing the established order, but never quite do, are very common. Travellers have been known to turn up in highly ritualised societies in the midst of what they not unreasonably perceived to be full-scale revolution. Gluckman mentions an early French traveller to the Zulu, a Monsieur Delegorgue, whom he quotes:

> I have also seen the king's party and that of the opposition on the point of hurling themselves upon one another. I have seen that the voice of the despot is no longer heeded, and that a revolution could have exploded then and there had a single ambitious man come forward to profit by the indignation of the party opposed to the king. But what surprised me no less, was the order which succeeded the end of this kind of popular tribunal. (p. 127)

Gluckman takes the view that highly ritualised societies believe in a supernatural, mystical source for the origin of their ritual. Their ritual is thus 'carved in stone' in a way in which ritual, such as it is, in our society is not. This may or may not be. Nevertheless, Gluckman is moved to opine, sceptically or perceptively, according to your point of view (1966):

> Yet I am also sometimes tempted to regard as 'ceremonies' other squabbling actions in our social life, which are usually assumed to be realistic. Parliamentary debates and election campaigns are full of dispute: I wonder how realistic much of this is, and what relation it bears to the actual taking of political decisions. (p. 135)

CONCLUSION

It's possible that Japan has gone too far one way and that Western society too far the other. Finding a middle course is what is needed. Be this as it may, it's worth ending this section by re-asserting that Japanese youth has been able to exit childhood and enter adolescence more or less effortlessly in relation to their Western counterparts. I believe the reason for this has been the Japanese cultural propensity towards continuously reinforced status definition. Introducing status definition, or re-introducing it, to Western society, within our own cultural perspective, will be a very small price to pay for such a rich reward.

Part VI

The Power of Ritual and Myth

THE THREE FATES OF CLASSICAL MYTHOLOGY

These arbitrarily controlled birth, life and death. By the way they behave, many youth in Western society seem to be tempting the Fates or Destiny.

The Three Fates c.1670, Sebastiano Mazzoni (1611–78) © The Barber Institute of Fine Arts, University of Birmingham / The Bridgeman Art Library

21
Creating Ritual to Order

If one wanted to, is it possible to create ritual to order? This is a question that has exercised, among many others, the British theatre director and children's writer James Roose-Evans and the American community psychologist David Blumenkrantz quoted above. Both men are aware of the power of ritual. Life lacking in ritual, they might agree, is impoverished. Absence of ritual is a recipe for confusion and uncertainty.

Roose-Evans was ordained into the Anglican Church in 1981. As a priest he would doubtlessly prefer people to immerse themselves in time-tested Christian rites, but he seems to understand that these rites, and those of other world religions, hold increasingly less sway in the modern world. He writes:

> Too many ancient rituals have lost contact with the deity. The virtual disappearance of rites of passage from our culture, together with a decline in the respect accorded to sacred ceremonial, has disconnected us from the archetypal imperatives which seek to transform our lives, and has left us without a mythic context to give them meaning. (1994, p. 2)

Roose-Evans doesn't believe it's possible to construct, or reconstruct, universal ritual:

> I do not believe that any one person can devise a rite of passage that would work for everyone! Such rituals evolve over time, taking centuries even, as evidenced in the major religions. (Private correspondence).

This is an important issue. Conceiving a programme for *all* adolescents is precisely the intention of this enterprise. From a practical point of view, there is no evidence, in societies which practise rite of passage, that the rite of passage is tailor-made to the child. Rite of passage is 'one-size-fits-all'. Those that 'don't fit' succumb. Furthermore, in these societies, if the child wishes to graduate to young adult status, and all the evidence is that most children ardently wish to do so, they must, and do, submit themselves without reservation, or publicly vented reservation, to all that is demanded of them. Roose-Evans does believe however that it is possible to generate personal and (small) group rituals. Not only is it possible, but hugely beneficial.

22
The Meaning of Ritual and Myth

Ritual and myth: beyond theatre

Stage effects are vital to theatrical success. Roose-Evans lists 11 important elements: numbers, place, space, time, costume, properties, design, choreography, text, lighting and sequel or follow-up. These tools by themselves are no more than nuts and bolts of good theatre, but ritual is beyond theatre: ritual is 'purposeful activity' (La Fontaine, 1985, p. 184), social action, status transformation, something which once performed thenceforth changes for good the structure of social organisation for actor, acted upon, and audience alike.

Roose-Evans refers to the loss of a 'mythic context' (1994, p. 2, as quoted above) to give meaning to the performance of ritual. For Blumenkrantz, this is a real problem. Myth is all important, bringing ritual to life. Without myth, we have no stories to tell our children; no reason to require them to perform ritual. The question for Blumenkrantz, and perhaps for us too, is not whether ritual can be created but whether myth can be created? Ritual is end product, myth is cause – ritual is dependant on myth.

Eight attributes of myth

The Concise Oxford Dictionary gives five definitions of myth of which two are of special concern to us:

> 1. a traditional narrative usually involving supernatural or imaginary persons and often embodying popular ideas on natural or social phenomena etc
>
> [...]
>
> 3. a widely held but false notion. (1998, p. 900)

For myth to have meaning, power and influence, its storyline must be believed; more importantly, it must be accepted to 'embody popular ideas on natural' or, very important for our purpose, 'social phenomena'. Myth is true, not false. Blumenkrantz (1996) quotes Sharpe (1984) who in turn has collected the opinions of nine distinguished scholars to provide the following attributes of myth.

1. MYTHS AS STORIES

First, myths are stories in which characters act out drama. In story form, almost anything and everything is possible.

2. GODS AND DEMIGODS

Story myths involve superheroes, gods and demigods, serving as role models to elaborate cultural values, traditions and beliefs. In highly ritualised societies, as we have seen with the Maasai, storytelling is still a rich ingredient in tribal life. Storytelling in Africa is an art. Stories are by no means told only to children; adults too are mesmerised by professional storytellers. Once told, stories are digested, discussed and deliberated upon. In highly ritualised societies, stories have never lost their adult appeal. They're the soap operas of daily life with the same hold on their societies as *EastEnders* and *Coronation Street* have on ours.

3. PREHISTORY

Myths are often set in prehistory where anything and everything was and is possible. 'Way back in dreamtime ...' begin the myths of Australia's aboriginal communities. Eliade (1957) has called this dreamtime '*illo tempore*', a kind of 'once upon a time'. To this extent, credible myth must be buried in history. You can commune with history, but history, in modern Western society at least, cannot commune with you. One recalls with a wry smile, the observation of the philosopher psychiatrist Thomas Szasz:

> If you say you are talking to God, you are praying;
>
> If you say God is talking to you, you have schizophrenia.

The implication is that modern Western scepticism holds that if you believe the Almighty is really talking to you, you need to consult a man in a white coat!

When a story is pitched in non-verifiable prehistory, its veracity is unchallengeable. It is possible, however, to construct a story in relatively modern times and then, with the elasticity of the human mind, to claim an ancient provenance for this story. Knight (1985) has noted just this for Freemasonry.

> Some Freemasons claim great antiquity for Freemasonry [...] Modern Masonic historians are far more cautious. It is now accepted that Freemasonry as practised today goes back little more than three centuries. What is true, though, is that the philosophic, religious and ritualistic concoction that make up the speculative element in Freemasonry is drawn from many sources – some of them, like the Isis-Osiris myth, dating back to the dawn of history (pp. 15–16).

Where actual practice commenced little more than 300 years ago but the sources are buried in prehistory it's convenient perhaps to blend the two.

4. Ordered experience

Myth orders experience (Barbour, 1974). Myths are a way by which man informs himself, or is informed, about himself.

5. Myth and morality

Eliade (1960) notes how myths serve as models for behaviour, both good and bad! Furthermore, myths stay in place for eternity and thus underpin the culture and cultural mores of a community.

6. Eternity

Eliade (1963) notes how myths strike deep into the emotional consciousness of the individual. He or she lives and relives the saga. The *Haggadah*, the story of the exodus from Egypt, recited by Jews at the annual Passover festival, requires that:

> Everyone, in all generations, should feel as if he personally had come forth from Egypt; for it is said (Exodus 13: 8), 'And thou shalt tell thy son on that day, saying, This is because of that which The Lord did for *me* when I came forth from Egypt.' It was not only our fathers that The Holy One, blessed be he, delivered: he redeemed *us too*, when he redeemed them.

7. Myth as living reality

Myth is 'living reality' (Sharpe 1984), as true today as ever before. Blumenkrantz (1997) quotes Eliade (1960) and asserts:

> Myths are accepted as true because of the belief that they narrate something as *really happened* and, as such, are re-enacted to bring them into present reality and reaffirm their authority. (p. 86)

8. BROUGHT TO LIFE THROUGH RITUAL

Finally, myths are 'brought to life' through the medium of ritual. Once again we should remind ourselves that the performance of ritual is more than the performance of theatre and drama: ritual is purposeful activity, aiming to affect the world; it's social action, potentially transforming the social status of *all* who witness it – actors, acted upon and audience alike.

23
A Myth for our Times

The question was asked in Chapter 21: can ritual be created? which leads to the question: can myth be created? The idea being that ritual is merely a means to enacting, or re-enacting, myth. Myth is the chicken, so to speak; ritual the egg.

The attributes of myth are fascinating. Every culture has its myths – know the myth, know the culture. Christian, Hindu, Islamic and Jewish culture cannot be understood without knowledge of the myths that predicate them. Moral lessons flow from these myths. The daily lives of millions of people are driven by norms deriving from them. The term myth is used here in the widest sense; it is not meant to offend.

But what of the many young people in Western society who know no myths, young people who don't subscribe to, or even know, the storylines of any great world religion? Youngsters who have gone haywire, who are hard-boiled, full of street-cred and cynicism, who all the time 'do their own thing'? What myth, what story, could ever be given to them whose commemoration, whose re-enactment would be acceptable? On the face of it: none. The creation of myth, mystery or mystique in a science-based, internet-linked, fully globalised world is, you might think, more impossible nowadays than it has ever been before.

But this is not in fact the case: a myth is in place. Adolescent lives in Western society are already ordered by this myth. Adolescents are performing ritual related to the myth day in and day out in their young lives. The myth is not yet explicit and its existence is by inference only. As with a new planet, it cannot be seen as such; the planet's influence on a nearby star reveals its existence. Continuing this analogy, the behaviour and actions adolescents adopt imply response to an underlying imperative. This imperative is our myth. It is whatever story lies behind the impulse of adolescents in every generation to want to walk out of the door marked 'exit to childhood' and travel along the corridor that ends with a door marked 'entrance to adulthood'.

Adolescents may, or may not, worship God as conceived in one or another of the great religions. They do however seem to propitiate Destiny, which may be an aspect of the supreme deity of whichever religion they follow; Destiny may be a goddess in her own right. It matters not. Most likely of all, Destiny is not (yet) thought of in conscious terms in any way whatsoever. But, by the actions they take, the behaviour they display, adolescents in Western society are to be seen 'dancing to Destiny's tune' almost every day of their young lives.

The myth takes shape and this is the story to tell every Western child:

There is in life a force. The force holds sway over young people's lives; particularly when they try to make the change from child to adult. We give this force a name. We call it Destiny, but you can give it any other name you like. Whatever you call it, it's there, ever-present in your life. Destiny is a goddess who plays like the Pied Piper of Hamelin, conducting mesmerised youngsters along the dangerous dark passage which lies between childhood's door marked 'exit' and adulthood's door marked 'entrance'. Nobody knows how Destiny works or why she does what she does.

While in the long dark passage, adolescents are under the goddess's merciless, capricious spell, in a similar way to the sinister entrancement of young Kay by the Snow Queen in Hans Andersen's fairy tale. No one escapes. The passage is full of pitfalls. Every so often Destiny spews a child out of the passage, dead, seriously injured or emotionally impaired. Young people 'squeeze along' the passage and eventually emerge, sometimes after many years. Some, often for the rest of their lives, are emotionally scarred by their experience, some physically scarred, some not at all. Those that make it to the end of the long passage are permitted to knock on the door marked 'entrance to young adulthood'. All who make it to the end of the passage are transformed, matured by the experience. All are *changed.* A new batch of young adults has been created.

This is the theme of the myth. It can be embellished as you please. But how does this myth fit the definitions provided above?

24
Youth as Dramatis Personae in the Destiny Myth

To the first point, that 'myths are stories in which characters act out drama', the story is all about what the goddess Destiny has in store for young people. Each adolescent is part of the myth; each has to enact his part as the myth unfolds especially for him or her. Adolescents are the dramatis personae who act out the ritual drama of adolescent misbehaviour which is unscripted, ad hoc and gratuitous.

We can change this, however. We cannot stop Destiny imposing her will on the young, but we can, and must, order the tune to which youngsters dance to her. Maybe by our doing so, Destiny can be made to wreak less havoc on the lives of vulnerable young people.

To the second point, that the myth should involve superheroes, gods and demigods, we have appointed a goddess whom youngsters must, and already do, propitiate. We have settled for naming her Destiny. Our goddess rules the long dark and dangerous passage between the exit from childhood along the entrance to adulthood. Her rule in this passage is unchallengeable, arbitrary and final.

To the third point, that myths are set in prehistory, in dreamtime, our myth fulfils this criterion. The goddess Destiny has been at work since the first human being was created.

The fourth point is that myth orders experience and is the means by which man is informed about himself. If our analysis is correct – that the deepest motivation for much of adolescent behaviour is that they are 'testing Destiny' – then, de facto, this is the myth which is already ordering experience and which has been doing so for a very long time. Moreover, by declaring this myth of the goddess Destiny and the power she exerts authentic, we can see adolescent misbehaviour in all its nefarious manifestations as no more than the ritual action by which this myth is acted out. Myth is the 'chicken'; ritual action 'the egg'. In this way of seeing things, man is indeed informing himself about himself. Each young person is out in the passage testing Destiny or tempting Destiny to test him or her. Adolescent (mis)behaviour is to be explained as ritual behaviour, designed to accelerate the advance of young adulthood.

According to this scenario an adolescent can, perhaps for the first time, understand why he is behaving the way he is: for example, surliness towards his family is saying he is opening the door marked exit from childhood and stepping out into the passage of Destiny; drug-taking, joy-riding, having unprotected sex, petty – and often not so petty – crime, are all just ways of testing Destiny or, alternatively, giving Destiny her chance to put upon him her capricious thumbs up or thumbs down.

On the fifth point, our myth is not a model for behaviour – not yet at any rate. Our myth is amoral. But with a course of ritual action designed to propitiate the goddess Destiny in a particular way, the arbitrary passage of Western youth into adulthood may yet be transformed into a model of exemplary behaviour which could constitute a true myth.

This Destiny myth fulfils the sixth criterion: it strikes deep into the emotional consciousness of the individual. Most individuals, most adolescents, would be prepared to accept that destiny, with or without a capital D, plays a crucial role in their lives. Some may refer to Destiny by another name; maybe they arrogate her role to that of a major deity or directly to God himself; but Destiny, by any name, impinges upon the consciousness of us all.

Finally, in response to the idea that myth is 'living reality', youth crime figures over the decades, seen in the light of the above points, prove the living reality of this myth. Arbitrary, ad hoc, spontaneous and ill-considered adolescent misbehaviour is thus elevated to ritual action, acting out of the Destiny myth. This point is made without in any way wishing to offend any reader who has personally, or whose relatives have, been the victim of vicious youth crime. Finding any justification, or making any excuse, for such behaviour could understandably be entirely unacceptable. But it is, after all, the ultimate objective of this exercise to put in place ideas and procedures which halt the progress of this terrible blight.

Part VII

The Rite of Passage Experience

From Crime of Passage to Rite of Passage

Youth of the future who have undergone rite of passage will be mature young adults: self-reliant, confident, assured of their position in the scheme of things and a great asset to society.

Photography: Track 5

25
Contemporary Rite of Passage

The idea that contemporary Western society lacks rite of passage for its youth is not original. The conclusion has already been reached; and there has been ensuing action. Theory has been translated into practice, which is praiseworthy when, so often, theory remains theory. The academic world is relatively secure: to forsake it to realise a vision is particularly courageous; especially when it means coping with the uncertainties and caprice of the private sector.

Dr David Blumenkrantz has founded the Center for the Advancement of Youth, Family & Community Services. The mission of the Center, which is based in Glastonbury, Connecticut, USA, is to promote positive youth development and assist children through adolescence and on to healthy adulthood. The Center describes its Rite of Passage Experience (ROPE) as its 'flagship' work (Internet extract). The acronym ROPE has been copyrighted and is protected against unauthorised use. The Center's website has been, and to date (2008) still is, accessible to computer users at www.rope.org.

The Center has adopted the Huichol Indian symbol of the hummingbird as its logo. For the Huichol Indians of New Mexico, the hummingbird is a symbol of transformation; she guides children to the door of the other world of adulthood – the place of power and knowledge to which they all eventually make pilgrimage. The Center's literature says that 'over one hundred thousand youth, families and community members nationwide have undertaken the Rite of Passage Experience' (ROPE) (Leaflet: The Center, Building Community the RITE way).

This raises the first obvious question: *why* families and community members when, surely, the Rite of Passage Experience is for youth, and for youth alone? This is not the case. Blumenkrantz is a community psychologist and his aim is to see communities live as communities. Communities that are not living as communities are in a betwixt and between state; Blumenkrantz follows the social scientist Victor Turner in calling this betwixt and between state *communitas*. A *communitas* is thus a body of people living together – but not really *living* together; people living dysfunctionally, not in any meaningful sense of community. There are plenty of neighbourhoods all over the world, particularly in urban environments, where *communitas* prevails over community.

CREDO

Blumenkrantz's credo is set out in his book: *The Rite Way – Guiding Youth to Adulthood and the Problem of Communitas*. Unfortunately, the book is available only as a PhD dissertation thesis (UMI Dissertation Services, Ann Arbor, Michigan). The price is high and acquiring a copy is time-consuming but not impossible. One day, it is to be hoped, this fascinating and pioneering work will be readily available in bookshops all over the world.

DAGARA FUNERAL RITUAL

Blumenkrantz believes in the authority, the imperative even, of personal experience. It is never right, he believes, to take people where you haven't yourself been before. To learn more of the power and nature of rite, he has on a number of occasions voluntarily submitted himself to its traumatic experience: he describes his participation in a Dagara funeral rite. The Dagara live in Burkino Faso, West Africa.

The 55 Western participants are organised by Professor Malidoma Some, a shaman in the Dagara tradition but also a widely acclaimed Western scholar with PhDs from the Sorbonne and Brandeis University, author (1993) of *Ritual: Power and Healing and Community* and (1994) *Of Water and the Spirit*. For Professor Some, grief is 'unfinished business'; and there is unfinished business in every unsuccessfully concluded relationship. Such a relationship can be with someone still living or someone who has died. Continuing grief must be given a proper funeral; only then will it melt away.

Blumenkrantz's recollection of this rite (1996, p. 114) is worth reproducing. The trauma and the catharsis the rite generates is truly breathtaking. Perceptively, he realises the significance of the (American) location chosen for the rite: the re-creation hall in a re-treat centre (it's amazing how the elemental meaning of a word can be lost by frequent verbalisation and accent shift). Professor Some organises the participants into clans – each with its own responsibility. He then supervised the building of the shrine, which is surrounded by candles; incense is introduced. Blumenkrantz quotes Some:

> Once this shrine is charged with the smoke, it is alive, I can not know what will happen. We must be careful and do exactly as I have instructed. The power is immense: it can draw you into it. Once, I remember a man drenched in his sorrow, abandoned his senses and plunged into the abyss, never to be seen again. I can't promise this won't happen again. Please – you must do your job and help me keep us safe. (p. 112)

Blumenkrantz's reaction to this was as follows.

> I couldn't believe what my ears had heard. Yet, instinctively I knew it to be true. My conscious mind was losing the battle for logic as the linear world began to drift away. I had a most peculiar feeling in the pit of my stomach. 'All things are possible,' I thought, 'if you let the experience enter in.'

The build-up is slow. All the men are together at one end of the hall, labelled 'the village'. No man is allowed to approach the smoking shrine at the other end of the hall by himself. It is deemed too dangerous and he has to be accompanied by protectors. Their job is to stop him throwing himself into the shrine as one would stop an overwrought mourner throwing themselves into a grave. Blumenkrantz is a protector.

The rite extends itself for over three hours to a tremendous climax:

> The slow flow of men approaching the shrine began to elevate in pace and intensity. Each disbursement of grief begot another of heightened intensity. Men began to charge up to the shrine, their anxious protectors frantically trying to guard their charge's every move. They cursed and screamed, directing their emotional declarations to a lover who scorned them, a spouse who divorced them, a father or mother who wasn't available for them, and an abundance of other sorrows they had labored to carry. I was astonished at the growing intensity and voracity of the men's deliveries. Some men laid down, prostrate on the floor, kicking and screaming, sobbing uncontrollably. Several men abandoned their clothes and repeatedly charged into the shrine, demanding that their protectors and I physically restrain them.
>
> The scene elevated to pandemonium. Groups of men approached the shrine in packs, screaming and crying as they delivered their grief and mourned their losses, their abandonment, their failures, consumed by their sorrows, awash in their pain. 'You left me, you bitch,' one man screamed into the abyss, tears screaming down his contorted face. 'You took everything I had – my money, my children, my house my heart – you took everything, even my manhood – you left me with nothing, you fucking bitch. (pp. 114–15)

Blumenkrantz describes how the men scream and cry in wild fury while he and their protectors desperately try to keep them from being sucked into the shrine. Gradually, very gradually, the frenzy subsides. After three full hours everybody is back in the village where they are formally received.

He also notes a very important point almost as an aside: the work of initiation is individual while responsibility for its transformative potential belongs to the community. He also quotes Some who incisively observes: 'A village is a village because it is held together by a shrine.'

We talk about the village church. A village is not a village unless it has a church. A church binds the village community together. The rites of passage of birth, marriage and death will be commemorated in the village through the rites of the church. And many other rites too. A village (unless half of it is taken over with holiday houses) is truly held together by its church. Ideally, a town will be an aggregation of villages each with its own (parish) church; a city, the same, but on a larger scale. Ideally, too, a balanced life will be a mixture of spirituality and materialism. While this may be the ideal, reality is very different. In many lives, spirituality has been all but eliminated; reduced to an occasional visit to church, once a decade or so, to attend a funeral. The question is: what constitutes a shrine?

Maybe there are other shrines, material shrines: temples of Mammon (shopping malls), clubs and societies. Can they, in Professor Some's terms, hold the village together? The answer is a matter of opinion. Many people in highly technological less-ritualised societies lead out their lives in a largely material environment: the company of family and friends, weekly shopping, the golf or football club, cultural activities, holidays and television – these all unite to make a not unpleasant life in which a spiritual shrine, as such, is not missed.

But if this is the case, why is there so much dysfunction? Why, so often, does *communitas* prevail over community? The answer is surely that few of these institutions are sustained by any form of philosophy which is remotely capable of giving succour in times of trouble and trauma or in times of ill-health. Family and friends certainly can and do give help. But, in a cultural environment which favours the small (nuclear) rather than extended family, too many people are left on their own to fend spiritually, if not materially, for themselves.

Few people are without worry at least some times in their lives. It is in times of anxiety that the spiritual shrine comes into its own. It has in its armoury, as Prof. Some's specially adapted Dagara funeral rite illustrates, the wherewithal to assuage individual ills. No Temple of Mammon or golf club or television programme is remotely able to fulfil this need. They are part of the equation. A shrine is the other part. One without the other is not enough. Life without a shrine, or access to one when needed, is life led in *communitas*.

HUICHOL INDIAN VISION-QUEST AND THE BARMITZVAH

Blumenkrantz is a glutton for punishment. In his early forties, he embarks upon another ritual experience, undergoing a vision-quest according to the rites of the Huichol Indians. A vision-quest is a journey undertaken physically and mentally; it may be taken alone or in company. If taken alone, as it was on this occasion, it is an opportunity to engage in introspection and self-analysis. One can never be sure exactly what is going to happen. The wanderings of the mind are tempered by the demands of the body for food and warmth, demands which must inevitably be attended to.

The meanderings of his mind on the lonely Virginian hilltop move Blumenkrantz to recall the trauma of his own barmitzvah, the ceremony at 13 on reaching the age of Jewish majority, which I discussed earlier in Chapter 16.

> Mr Gruttman, a short man with large glasses and thinning hair, spoke with an accent, uttering words that leaped back at me thirty years later with all the power they had at that moment. With a degree of seriousness fit for the disclosure of a terminal illness to a patient, he firmly stated to my parents 'David's not ready.' I saw the shock on my mother's face. Her eyes opened wide, lips parted emitting an audible gasp as she reached out towards my father. 'What do you mean he's not ready? We've booked the caterer and reception hall!' she meekly exclaimed searching for some kind of response. My father looked at me shaking his head. My eyes dropped to the floor. (p. 47)

Readers need not worry. Barmitzvah boys have a habit of shaping up at the last minute. The barmitzvah boy was OK on the day – exemplary even:

> My voice is strong, the congregation is silent, their eyes are upon me. I am their emissary, they have entrusted me with the honour of continuing the cycle begun many millennium [*sic*] before. The reading ends, the congregation signals in unison 'Amen'. It is done. With that single word 'Amen', they have affirmed my status as their emissary, fulfilling the community's responsibility to continue the heritage of Abraham, Isaac and Jacob. (pp. 47–8)

Armed with their Sacred Prayer Arrows, blessed by the Mara Akame, the Huichol Indian Shaman, and clothed in ceremonial attire, 25 human beings, Blumenkrantz included, depart along the Pocahantas Trail into the million acre Cranberry Mountain Preserve in Hillsboro, West Virginia. Each individual will leave the beaten track to find his own place; there, to spend a week in total solitude to commune with the gods, the spirits, the universe and, above all, himself; the warmth of the sun by day, the warmth of the fire by night; no watch, no radio, no contact of any kind – the passage of time is marked by a daily notch on a rock.

The Huichol Indian vision-quest went according to plan. Blumenkrantz communed with nature and enjoyed a journey of introspective self-discovery. Less enjoyable was the journey back. He got thoroughly and somewhat dangerously lost. In the end, dishevelled and disoriented, he regained the village as did, eventually, all the other participants.

26
WHAT CONSTITUTES A RITE OF PASSAGE?

These stories of Blumenkrantz's personal involvement in ritual have been reproduced for a reason. They neatly introduce the question: what constitutes a rite of passage? This question is considered now within the context of our main theme: exit from childhood and entrance to young adulthood. Why is this question so important? It is important because one wants to preclude the possibility of an authority attempting to label or validate an activity as a rite of passage when it is not even a rite, let alone a rite of passage; when the activity is just an activity, an ad hoc event.

For a rite of passage to be a rite of passage, three conditions must be fulfilled:

1. THERE MUST BE RITE

What is rite? In Chapter 10, the dictionary definition for 'ritual' was given as 'a procedure regularly followed'. Perhaps we should add the words: 'to advance a spiritual requirement'. In this lies the subtle difference between the two nouns rite and ritual: rite is activity advancing a spiritual purpose; ritual on the other hand may refer to activity which is secular: rising in the morning at a particular time, for example, may be said to be part of a person's ritual. Observing the courtesies of life, saying 'Hello', 'Good morning' and 'How are you?' is ritual as opposed to rite.

Perhaps a little confusing however is that the word 'ritual' is also the adjectival form of the word 'rite'. In its adjectival form, we talk about 'ritual meal', 'ritual symbolism' and 'ritual prayer' etc. An activity may be neither rite nor ritual. It can simply be ad hoc, such as jumping on a bus to get from 'a' to 'b', or going on holiday. An activity may therefore be examined on three counts:

a) is it ad hoc – neither rite nor ritual?

b) if it's not ad hoc, is it ritual or rite?

c) if it's rite, is it rite of passage? Saying grace before and after meals, for example, is a rite but not a rite of passage.

Returning specifically to our main theme, if a rite of passage, like an academic course, is to be delivered in segmented units, there must be rite (regularly followed procedure/s) attendant upon each unit. These 'regularly followed procedures' should be public and recorded. The rite may be verbal (prayer or invocation); physical (body movement); dress (anything from wearing a badge to putting on a complete special outfit) or a mixture of two or all three.

Rite must never be 'casualised'. Rite is part and parcel of the process of an individual's social change. Only by the performance of publicly approved rite can an individual be successfully translated from one social status to another. I recall (yet again) La Fontaine's insights (above, Chapters 9 and 10): rite is 'purposeful activity'; rite aims to 'affect the world': subjectively the world of the participant and objectively the world of all those who witness the ritual performance.

For example, a child or a group of children may be required to undertake a journey as part of, or culmination to, their rite of passage. Such a journey must be distinguished from being 'any old journey', a simple holiday. There are many ways this can be done. The distinctions, whatever they are, will be drafted and conceived to emphasise the journey's function as part of, or culmination to, a comprehensive rite of passage.

A further example: Jews welcome in the Sabbath and festivals in their homes with formal sanctification (*kiddush* prayer). Wine is poured into a ceremonial goblet. The goblet is always supplied with a special plate to stand it on. There is no obvious purpose for the plate save to distinguish the sanctification goblet from any other goblet or wine glass that could easily be used. This is its ritual role.

Summing up: rite must be identifiable. The ritual manifestation of rite may be in words, action or dress; but words, action or dress must be plainly on show for all to see. Rite of passage must be universal. For a rite of passage to be accepted and to be regarded as credible, it must apply, and be applied, to all members within the group. In the case of a rite of passage converting children into adults, the group is the whole society and all children in it. There must be passage.

'Passage' means translation from one (publicly) recognised social status to another: exit from childhood and entrance to adulthood. If a body administering a rite of passage is not in a position, for whatever reason, to grant passage, then there has been no rite of passage. For a body to be able to grant passage, it must preside over the doctrine to which all members of the body subscribe. Only then is it in a position to confer status within the confines of the doctrine. Thus, a religious body has the power to initiate and confirm believers; Freemasons to initiate new members; while a secular body, the state, arbitrates upon the secular status of its subjects. This applies to making men out of boys and conferring the necessary change in status. A government is of course perfectly able and perfectly entitled to delegate its powers.

THE DAGARA FUNERAL RITE

Blumenkrantz states of the Dagara funeral rite: 'I did not know for certainty why I was there. In my exploration into human phenomenon, I engage in divergent activities in the hope of achieving some keen insight to enhance my work' (1996, p. 106). He thought he was going to receive from Prof. Some, in company with others, a seminar about ritual. The reality turned out to be very different.

This raises the question whether rite can be transferred willy-nilly from one culture to another; and if so, whether it can be effective. The Dagara rite, we are told (1996, p. 105), was specially 'crafted' by Prof. Some from the Dagara culture's funeral customs and 'extended' to Western men. The participating Americans could not have got more out it if they were themselves Dagara. They went to 'bury their grief'; to 'conclude unfinished business'. And this is what they seem to have done. To answer the question, it seems that a rite can be extrapolated from one culture to another. But the process of extrapolation must be conducted with care and sensitivity.

Blumenkrantz himself had no grief to bury. He was there as an observer; he ended up as a helper, physically to prevent the overwrought from doing themselves bodily harm. Insofar as he witnessed and experienced the rite, he was obviously deeply affected; he was very much a participant.

In a point very strongly made in the previous chapter, rite is not theatre: there is no audience. Celebrants and witnesses are equally participant – each role validated, reinforced by the other. Whether in the cultural original version of the rite, the Dagara celebrants receive any form of formal status-change, any passage for burying their grief, I do not know. In this Western version of the ceremony, we see rite – but without passage. The same may be said of the Huichol Indian vision quest – rite, without passage.

Barmitzvah is different: it is transformative – 'for the first time I realise that I am someone among them' (1996, p. 48) – and truly a rite of passage. For the first time, Blumenkrantz qualifies to be a member of the

Orthodox Jewish quorum of ten adult males. Religious privileges ensue. Passage is however limited. It is limited to the strict confines of Orthodox rite. No-one suggests that a 13-year-old boy, outside the confines of the religious quorum, is in any way adult. In a secular environment he is still a child with a lot to learn.

27
ROPE

THE RITE-OF-PASSAGE EXPERIENCE

Blumenkrantz's Center for the Advancement of Youth, Family and Community Services does not deliver a uniform rite-of-passage programme. To understand why, we return to the point made at the beginning of Chapter 25: Blumenkrantz is a community psychologist. His Center is not just interested in youth; it is interested in the 'village' as an whole. His primary emphasis is therefore on the village, not on rite of passage. His objective is to galvanise the village. If the village is up and running, this is a plus. Where he finds communitas, as opposed to community, there is extra hard work to do. In both cases the work is the same. This work is summed up in the heading of one of the pieces of literature sent out to prospective clients and headed:

> **Building a Collaborative Community through Rites of Passage**

The Rite of Passage Experience is therefore a means to an end, not an end in itself. As stated, there is no uniform rite-of-passage programme:

> ...the goal is to empower communities to *create and implement their own rites of passage* [my emphasis] through a combination of contemporary social science technology and traditional wisdom. (Center literature, April 2001)

The Center sees its role as advisory. Its objective is to get members of a community together and, having got them together, get them thinking for themselves. The Center is able to offer advice based on sound philosophy and years of grass-roots experience. But at the end of the day, the programme a particular community implements will be its own, not the Center's, which is exactly what the Center wants.

The Center's philosophy is both simple and profound – a rallying-cry for our times. It is founded upon the ancient Ashanti proverb, 'it takes a whole village to raise a child'. The idea, in Western society, of the community as a whole taking part in child rearing is so disconnected from reality that it beggars belief. The proverbial ideal that most pervades public consciousness is that children should be seen and not heard. As for villages, the English village of Yarnfield in Staffordshire symbolises today's reality: it takes a whole village to tame and suppress its children

YARNFIELD, STAFFORDSHIRE, JULY 2004: A TALE OF OUR TIMES

In July 2004, Yarnfield made the headlines: 'HOW ONE VILLAGE ROSE UP AGAINST THE 11 TEENAGE YOBS WHO MADE LIFE HELL' was the full-page banner headline in the *Daily Mail* (27 July). A gang had been terrorising the village for 18 months. The teenage members of the gang were sons and daughters of the village. Their parents were comfortably off, hard-working, middle-class members of the community: a businessman, an accountant, a farmer and an engineer were among their number.

Villagers worked together and prevailed upon the borough council and the police. These two bodies, at the villagers' behest, were eventually successful in obtaining ASBOs (antisocial behaviour orders) from the local Cannock Magistrates Court against individual gang members. The action, according to the newspaper report, cost the British taxpayer £60,000. So many of Yarnfield's 1000 residents attended court that more chairs had to be brought in to seat them all.

Private investigators had been hired by the council to help the villagers gather evidence. Eighteen months of teenage unruly behaviour were diarised. This behaviour included trespassing and damaging people's property; using foul, abusive and sexually explicit language; throwing stones, eggs and fruit; blocking traffic; spitting, urinating and throwing litter in the street; and driving motorbikes around the village recklessly.

IT TAKES A WHOLE VILLAGE TO RAISE A CHILD

We return to the work of the Center for the Advancement of Youth, Family and Community Services in Glastonbury, Connecticut, whose director made the following profound insight:

> The celebration of a rite of passage is renewing for the entire community. A child's public expression of and commitment to a community's values, attitudes and beliefs reinforces those important elements for the entire community. A child's coming of age presents an opportunity for the whole community to examine and re-commit themselves to their social and cultural heritage. In this light, *it takes a whole child to raise a village* [my emphasis]. (Blumenkrantz, 1996, p. 21)

In the Center's view, a community that actively engages in raising its children continuously renews and sustains itself. Moreover, the relationship is reciprocal. What the community does for the child, the child more than pays back to the community. The mutual relationship therefore confers benefit upon (a) the child, (b) its parents and (c) the community.

A THREE-PHASE, SIX-YEAR PROCESS

The Center has a core philosophy integrated into a concrete programme which is structured into a three-phase, six-year process. The Center has pioneered a further breakthrough: it has produced a template for the personnel roles need to carry out its ROPE (Rite of Passage Experience) programme. These include: parent/s (of course); school and community-agency representatives; mentorship relationships and peer counselling. This combination of roles ideally supports each child during his progress through the programme. Similar support is given to Maasai children, and the children of many other cultures too, as they prepare for their transition (see Part IV, above).

The three phases reflect the tripartite structure of a rite-of-passage ritual as detailed by van Gennep (see Chapter 12): separation, transition and re-integration. The three phases are not necessarily in equal segments.

PHASE 1: AMERICAN GRADE 6 – CHILDREN AGED 11–12

Phase 1 (1996, p. 200) focuses on separation of child from primary school and impending separation of child from parents. Programmes which build life-skills are delivered to the children. What these life-skills may be is not precisely clear, but the Center claims they help the children 'build their self-esteem and resiliency' (literature extract):

Blumenkrantz states in his main work (1996) that orienteering skill is a powerful first step towards self-esteem and resilience. One example of a life-skill a child will be taught will certainly be the ability to read and use a compass. Programme content is generally not outlined in detail, because it varies all the time, as each ROPE client is required to develop its own programme. Center advice and experience are always to hand, but there is no question of a community being shoe-horned into a one-size-fits-all uniform programme. Many roads lead to Rome: each of the Center's community clients is counselled – required even – to create its own way.

> [...] the curriculum, once contextualised to the specific site, also provides a vehicle to introduce important ingredients for having healthy fun, thus setting the stage for the next phase.

Phase 2: Transition stage – children of 13–15

The transitional stage: this focuses on connecting young people with community resources. The Center's literature states:

> pooled energy and resources of school personnel and community create opportunities for young people to meaningfully participate in positive leisure-time activities, guiding them towards pro-social community involvement.

The child is encouraged to understand that he is embarking on a process of personal transformation. The Center wants to see a 'shift in consciousness', a connection to 'spiritual self'. Once again, precise details of recommended activities are thin on the ground, but such activities as are outlined include: rope courses, rock-climbing, rappelling, vision-quest and 'other solo experiences' (1996, p. 201).

These activities embody complementing qualities: individual resilience on the one hand; team participation and team support on the other. Great emphasis is made by the Center of the concept of positive play, which is contrasted with its alternative, self-destructive activity. Drinking, drug abuse and sexual experimentation are put forward as examples of self-destructive activity. Blumenkrantz (1996) sees play as a substitute, the only substitute, to ritual:

> I recognize that certain individuals may be puzzled by some of the central initiatives within the Rite of Passage Experience and wonder how they relate to traditional activities and their symbols. Let me take a moment to try and briefly relate to several broad areas that address this issue. First, the second phase of the Rite of Passage Experience relates to having fun or play. This is built on the foundation set in the first phase where youth are engaged in challenging activities requiring considerable effort, thinking, co-operation, practice, problem-solving, trust and personal confidence. Over the past fifteen years tens of thousands of youth have participated in these activities and ninety-five per cent of youth reported these activities to be fun, enjoyable or as one youth said, 'the best thing to come along since comic books'. They have deeply experienced the art of having fun and play. (p. 207)

He continues:

> Play is closely related to spirituality. *It may be the only activity we can promote in a secular, public agency or school without being run out of town* [my emphasis]. Play and having fun are important elements in a well balanced life. In today's high paced world, full of a myriad of distractions, the art of play is being lost. (p. 208)

The quotation above linking ROPE's work to comic books is somewhat facile. Blumenkrantz does himself a disservice in reproducing it. A Maasai youth would be unlikely to regard his rite of passage in such a trivial way. ROPE's research, as we shall see, produces much better material than this to endorse its contribution.

The question of myth and ritual has been extensively considered in Part VI above. I do not share Blumenkrantz's assumption that ritual cannot be promoted 'in a secular, public agency or school without being run out of town'. For the moment, the advantage, however, lies with Blumenkrantz. He has the on-the-ground experience. His programme is operational, whereas mine is for the time being speculative and theoretical.

Phase 2: Transition stage – more details

Once again you should remember that ROPE works by encouraging its clients to work out their own salvation. There is no imposed programme. ROPE will present ideas and each client body will give expression to these ideas in its own way. ROPE provides the framework; the client body puts meat on the bones!

In this context, youth are encouraged to build up personal skills. They are encouraged to use these skills in settings that afford them higher status as an emerging adult in the community. The parallel would be the adolescent Maasai who shows he can use his herding stick to corral the herd.

The public demonstration of the acquired skill can be made the occasion for celebration: a ritual dinner at which an award is made; a new stage of ROPE embarked upon.

ROPE is keen on participants gaining cultural and ethnic awareness, subjectively and objectively, and sees mentorship relationships as important. Community elders mentor the older adolescents; while the older adolescents mentor new recruits entering the initiatory process. This latter technique mimics tribal practice.

Who is a community elder? Anyone prepared to serve as a role model. The words 'elder' and 'age' do not necessarily, in this context, have anything to do with each other. Anyone who feels able, or is thought able and willing to respond, to give help – 'leadership' is too strong a word – may be styled a community elder.

The ROPE programme attracts community elder volunteers. Getting everybody to sing from the same hymn sheet is another problem.

PHASE 3: INCORPORATION, CHILDREN – 15–17

If the transition period was a time to learn about life, this is a time to get involved. The Center is in no doubt what this means: 'the important adult value of giving one's self to others through community service' (ibid., p. 206). This work, Blumenkrantz believes, will help adolescent awareness of (a) parenthood and its responsibilities; (b) life in a democracy (the USA) which requires participation; and (c) respect for the Earth from an ecological point of view.

Acting as mentors to incoming initiates starting phase 1 of the enterprise is part of giving of oneself to others, together with helping students in some of their phase 2 transitional activities. Assistance from recent graduates, 'near peers', encourages involvement in ROPE.

28
ROPE's Impact

Research Results

The Center conducts intensive research into its own effectiveness. The results are published in the Center's literature and in greater detail in Blumenkrantz's major work (1996) already cited. Reaction comes from three sources: the community institutions that commission for themselves a ROPE initiative; parents of children involved in ROPE; young people themselves.

Young people' comments

Taking the latter first, what better accolade than the words of Kirby Reutter of Tolland, Connecticut who responded to a ROPE questionnaire in April 1992:

> R.O.P.E. has truly showered down a great experience upon me, an experience I feel every sixth-grader across the nation should have. It was here that my personal qualities unknown to even myself were revealed, and here where we learned the simple art of trusting, encouraging and cooperation with our much-needed peers.
>
> At R.O.P.E. we were taught that no hurdle is too massive to jump, and likewise, no goal, no problem, and no challenge in life is too massive to solve or fulfil as long as we put forth the required effort and patience.
>
> Through the course of the session, we, as students, were also informed that there is no way of escape from life's obstacles, but instead we are provided many kind people in this world of ours, who are always willing to take us in, and of whom we may seek comfort, support and help.
>
> The skills I have learned in R.O.P.E. I will sincerely treasure to the end of this year, through adolescence, and furthermore into the future, even until my last days on earth. (Blumenkrantz, 1996, p. 219–20)

Shorter contributions from other children include:

- It helped me to get over some fears about teenage years
- ... to feel confident about yourself and tell yourself you can do it.
- I can make a decision and not worry about peer pressure; you don't follow other people just because they're your friends.
- I learned to work in a group and even with people I don't like.
- If you listen to others' ideas, you can come up with better answers
- I learned that I am useful and can be a big help in a problem

PARENTS AND TEACHERS' COMMENTS

Parents comments include:

- I think R.O.P.E. is a fantastic program. There should be more programs like this in the school system. It's a real life-learning situation.
- My son brought home his experiences and new knowledge every night after he had a R.O.P.E. class. And it was discussed for days after.
- I think R.O.P.E. is an excellent program and would like to see it continued. With this type of program the kids are learning while having fun. This is the first year my daughter insists on going to school even when she's ill. (reproduced on website)

Teachers report classroom benefits from ROPE:

- brainstorming, problem solving techniques carry over into the classroom;
- helps build self-esteem; children work cooperatively towards one goal;
- children achieve personal goals
- children looked forward to discussing their concerns with someone who would listen, understand and guide them. (website extract)

These attitudes were mirrored by quantitative evaluations: ROPE students were monitored against a control group. ROPE students increased their drug use by 2%; the control group by a massive 175% (website extract). Similar ratios in favour of ROPE were achieved in measuring: family involvement, attachment to school; and indulgence in delinquency behaviour.

THE COMMUNITY'S COMMENTS

The community is the Center's foremost target. Bringing about a psychological sense of community is the Center's ultimate goal. In this aim, the project appears to be very successful. One question of qualitative evaluation asks 'who did the project mobilise?' (Blumencrantz, 1996, p. 235)

- It basically mobilised everybody in our church in every category and demographic – it ranged from housewives working with professionals such as doctors, principals, teachers. You will find young people under the age of 13 and 14 working together with people over the age of 50 and 60. There was a wide demographic of people coming together and mobilising for the betterment of the community.
- This is the first program that the town ever coordinated together, we shattered barriers.
- The Core Group of elders is very reflective of the community. We have a good range of young and not so young people who have been in the town for a long time and people who have just moved into town and looking for a way to be part of the community.

Developing a core group of elders is essential to getting a ROPE project off the mark. It takes approximately 40 hours of training to build a core group (Blumenkrantz, article in Developing Competent Youth and Strong Communities through After-School Programming, eds: Steven J Danish and Thomas P. Gullotta, undated, p. 94).

The question of who constitutes an elder was briefly considered above. Suffice to say, elders may be formal or informal leaders originating from community-based agencies, school administrators and teachers, civic organisations, parents, police, clergy and recently graduated young people themselves. At the end of the day, 'elders' just know who they are, who is suitable and who is not and what qualities are needed. One interviewee stated:

- Generally, people who contain those qualities know it. When I was asked if I wanted to come, if I didn't contain those qualities, I would not have shown up. But because it was something I was interested in doing, I just did it. People who don't have those qualities would not show up. I don't know what kind of orientation you would give them. If the point of this is for kids to see what their elders are like or their youth elders are like, that's something that has to be brought across and I don't know how you train them for that. The people that contain those qualities, you see it by being with them. (ibid., p. 239)

- And another:
- You couldn't take the average person off the street, either people have those qualities or they don't and it's hard to instil them in someone.

Unquestionably the Center for the Advancement of Youth, Family & Community Services' ROPE programme is effective. In case there is any doubt, the Center's website points out:

> Perhaps most significant about these initiatives is that 3 years after state funding expired 80% of the initiatives continue to grow and serve the communities. Over 10,000 people became involved in the rites of passage initiatives and generated over $1 million of additional resources towards youth and community development.

Clearly, the Center is needed by the community and the Center's work has been well received by the community.

ROPE: A CRITICAL ASSESSMENT

1. PRACTICAL PROBLEMS

It is an invidious task to offer criticism of an enterprise that is so positive. Fortunately, the Center is aware of its own shortcomings. These may be divided into two: the theoretical and the practical. In a sense, both are completely beyond the control of the Center itself. To this extent, the Center is blameless; and is to be regarded as fighting the good fight against overwhelming odds.

In his 1996 opus, Blumenkrantz, the Center's founder and director, elaborates on his difficulties. On the practical side, first and foremost is funding. Funding bodies are notoriously capricious and chameleonic: they change name and, with name-change, they change policy too. He outlines the problem faced in one of the Center's initiatives: 'Paths to the Year 2000'. In less than two years, both the grant-making body and the separate grant supervising body underwent metamorphosis. All of this had a dramatic and deleterious effect on the project.

Blumenkrantz has had to learn the hard way. Politicians and civil servants are fickle. They hate and resist change. Platitudes are mouthed; but no-one is willing to put their money where their mouth is – especially when 'change' is predictable:

> in situations of major social change, the prevailing ground rules are likely to block the path to creative solutions of serious new problems. Creative solutions will depend upon the ability of the organization to change the organizational and intellectual ground rules (Whyte *et al.*, 1991, p. 42; quoted in Blumenkrantz, 1996, p. 262).

Blumenkrantz continues:

> Clearly the state [of Connecticut] was unprepared to 'walk the talk' and support a paradigm shift operationalized through their own grant to a local agency (the State Department of Mental Health and Addiction Services). While they articulated the need for a paradigm shift, they could not have fully considered nor practically accepted the consequences of a 'revolution' (Kuhn, 1970) in the way things are perceived and done. No bureaucracy wants to turn itself upside down, in spite of the potential benefits.

I have absolutely no doubt there will be similar reaction to my own proposals as they are advanced in the next section. Revolutionary change provokes fear. This is understandable and is to be anticipated. The status quo, currently so abhorrent and unattractive, will suddenly seem not so bad after all. That is human nature.

2. Theoretical Problems

It is on the theoretical side however that the Right of Passage Experience faces its most serious difficulty. Its own research (Blumenkrantz, 1996, p. 247) elaborates what this is. In answering research question no. 9:

> What is the hope you have about this project for other adults, children & yourself?

one of the interviewees responds:

> I would hope this actually does become a rite of passage. Because right now I don't think it is; it may build into one. I would really like to see it become a real rite of passage so a child expects that they have to pass through this to become an adult. I mean town wide, city wide; it's a good program. (ibid., p. 248)

The basic criteria for a rite of passage were discussed above. Through no fault of its own, ROPE fulfils none of the three criteria:

1) a) The programme is devoid of rite. This deficiency could possibly be addressed, but in the absence of ROPE's ability to deliver on the remaining two, it would for the moment be pointless to spend time on this matter.

b) The programme does not apply to all children – either in the State of Connecticut or in the United States as a whole. It is probably beyond the Center's wildest dreams that this could ever be the case. The Center may not yet appreciate that such a dream is conceivable; and how much of the groundwork it has already pioneered.

c) The programme cannot grant passage – which is held to mean 'change in personal status'. Without the intervention of the state, despite the Center's best endeavours, there can be no actual passage as such. Only the state, sanctioned by society as a whole, can control change in personal status. A genuine rite of passage must offer formal exit from childhood and formal entrance to adulthood. In the term 'Rite of Passage Experience', the keyword is the word 'experience' – with nuances of 'delving into', 'sampling', 'savouring', 'getting an idea of'. There is no idea of completion, of transformation.

Blumenkrantz sees his programme *evolving* into a 'true' rite of passage. It seems that one of his funding authorities, the Connecticut Alcohol and Drug Abuse Commission, sensed otherwise. Funding was unexpectedly withdrawn. The letter that Blumenkrantz writes to them, and which he reproduces, is very revealing:

> The creation of 'true' rites of passage initiatives, which reflect the initial program criteria for rites of passage, takes considerable effort, patience and time. It is unreasonable to expect a 'whole village to raise a child' within one or two years. There are a number of phases within the creation process. The initial phase, which we are presently in, focuses primarily on raising community awareness of the importance of rites of passage and the impact of its absence. We begin to develop programs which reflect the initial criteria used to describe the rite of passage concept. The next phase will be the continuation of awareness efforts while building a larger and broader coalition of the community to actively support the rite-of-passage project. Support should begin to increase both in active community participation in the project activities as well as financial support. The next phase should also include review, refinement and further development of

> program activities which move the projects closer to a true community rite of passage.
>
> I look forward to our continued 'collaborative evolutionary process' on behalf of mobilizing your community to create strong and true rites of passage. (ibid., p. 249)

Summary

In the absence of a proper rite of passage for Western youth, Dr David Blumenkrantz's Center for the Advancement of Youth, Family and Community Services and its Right of Passage Experience (ROPE) has attempted to do something unique in Western society. It may remain so for a long time to come. The deciding factor will be the extent to which Western governments accept that juvenile crime is 'crime of passage'; and that crime of passage and rite of passage are two sides of the same coin. At the moment, Western society is faced with looking at the wrong side of the coin. Whether the coin can be flipped over depends on to what extent the proposals outlined in Part VIII are viable and acceptable.

PART VIII

PASSAGE-TIME

PROPOSAL FOR A PRESENT-DAY RITE OF PASSAGE

Proposals for a Present-day Rite of Passage

Life-skills, life-experiences and voluntary service (mission challenge) are requirements for all candidates; included amongst these is a knowledge of first aid.

Photography: Jeanell Norvell

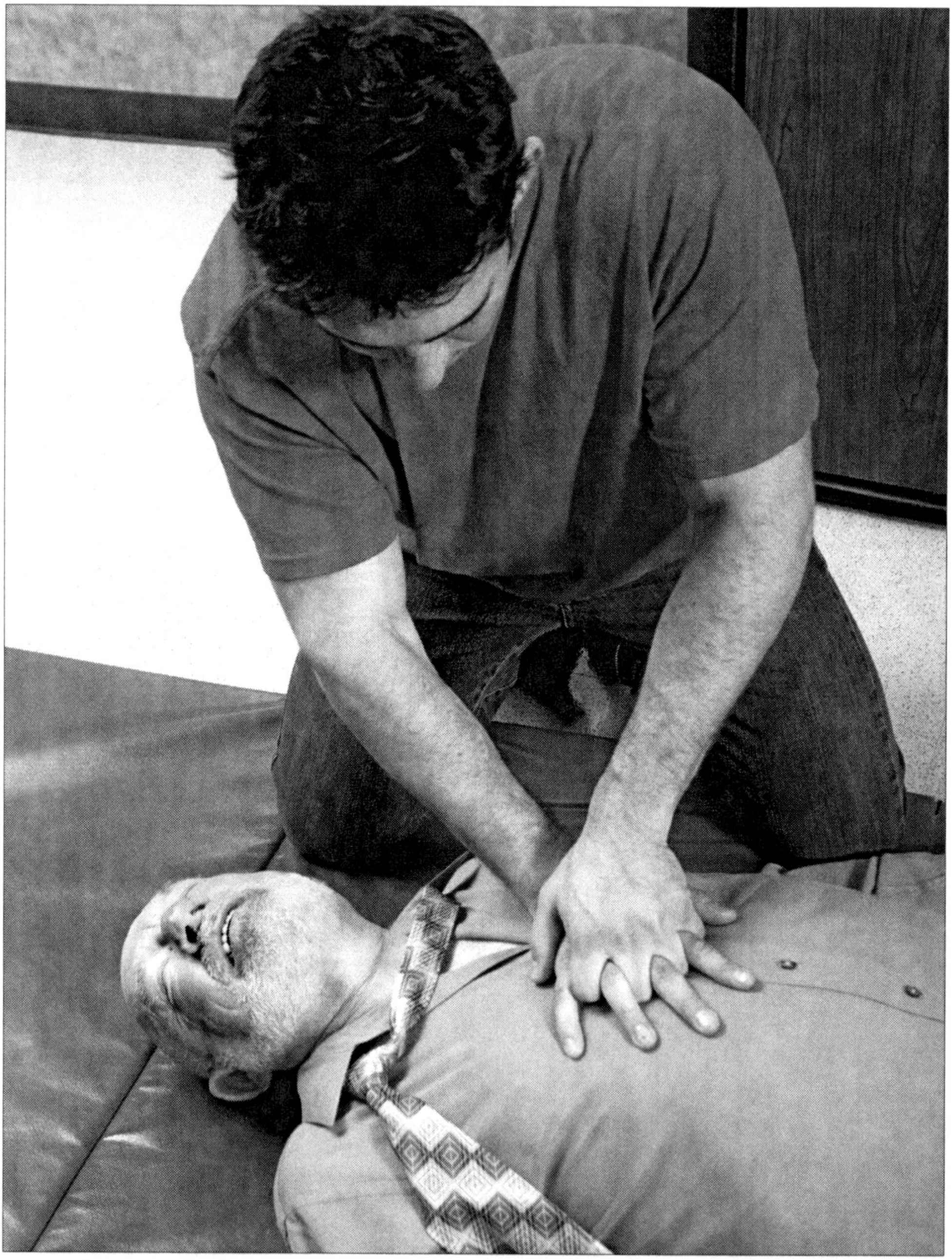

29
Review Of Parts I–VII

This section outlines a proposal for a present-day rite of passage. The proposal implements principles developed in previous chapters and therefore at this point a brief review of Parts I–VII is appropriate, concentrating on salient principles – those that provide the philosophical basis for the proposal.

Parts I–III

In Parts I–III (Chapters 1–12) of this book, I have proposed that the root cause of adolescent misbehaviour is Western society's failure to provide a social mechanism for children to exit childhood and enter adulthood. Recalling Shakespeare's famous monologue, 'All the world's a stage', childhood ('unwillingly to school...') and adulthood ('and then the lover...'), I argue, are two very separate life-stages. Highly ritualised societies acknowledge these life-stages and organise formal change between the two, while Western-type societies, up to now, do not. In the absence of an official state-organised exit/entrance programme, children develop their own ad hoc change-in-personal-status agenda, which is characterised by behaviour change, extending from mild fractiousness to sustained criminality. The issue for Western-type society crystallises into either planned rite of passage on the one hand or unplanned crime of passage on the other.

The question of social status lies at the very heart of the problem. This is the key: get this right and everything else falls into place. I also noted British newspaper reports referring to a study which concluded that men eventually mature around the age of 35 and women 30. This highlighted two points: (1) that juveniles do eventually mature; (2) that juveniles are not, except in rare cases, career criminals. This led to the conclusion that juvenile delinquency and adolescent misbehaviour are a means to an end, not an end in itself.

I point out the contrast between education and socialisation. Education per se, I argue, vital though it is, is not enough. The 'something else' that is required is a programme of socialisation. Education, I suggest, is intellectual; transition from one social status to another is not intellectual. Status transition is a social process and rite of passage is thus a process of socialisation, not education.

I propose a distinction between entertainment theatre and ritual drama. The two should not be confused. Ritual drama, superficially indistinguishable from entertainment theatre, transforms human beings from one social status to another. The transition in social status that particularly concerns us here is of course the transition from child to adult.

PARTS IV–VI

In Parts IV–VI I identify the three-part elements of traditional rite-of-passage: separation; transition ('passage'); reintegration. The transition middle stage is the key stage. This stage contains the rite-of-passage programme. Among the Maasai, this middle stage for young males comprises a lengthy build-up to circumcision. Performed without the palliatives of modern medicine, a small percentage, fewer than two per cent, succumb. Death in circumcision is a factor among all peoples who perform initiation in the traditional way.

I noted the reaction to such death and reproduce La Fontaine's quotation (1985, p. 98): 'I am sorry to tell you the pot you have given me to fire is broken' – the words a tribal elder uses to convey a boy's death to his family. I noted how such a boy is formally treated as if he never existed; how there is the belief that he has never been destined, or pre-destined, by the spirits to reach manhood.

I have examined Japanese practice in Part V. Japan is a highly ritualised society although she has no discernible rite of passage. Furthermore, the last five decades of the twentieth century saw a decline in Japanese crime figures (see Appendix 2) decline whilst Western youth crime figures increased dramatically during this period. The conundrum was resolved. The Japanese language provides the answer. Japanese as a spoken language decrees recognition of, and rigid obedience to, social status. Speaker and addressee have little linguistic choice. The process commences from the beginning of the ability to speak. It never lets up; except in the closest family context.

This phenomenon in Japanese language and culture confirms the fundamental speculation of this work: adolescent misbehaviour and ambiguity in social status are inextricably linked. Create certainty, eliminate ambiguity, and delinquency will recede of its own accord. This is a first principle.

Social status in Japan advances in small increments: a first-year student will defer to a second-year student and so on. The important factor is that every individual is accredited social status. Provided the rules for acquiring it are uniform, Japanese children and Japanese adolescents have no further worries. Japanese adolescents have no need to spend time acquiring new (adult) status. It is done for them. Japanese, the language, is the vehicle. Status acquisition, per se, is simply not part of their social agenda. In Western societies, the contrast could not be greater; adolescent life is frequently dominated by a drive to acquire adult, or what is thought to be adult, social status.

Part VI concentrates on the notion of destiny, which is elevated into the role of a goddess whose caprice holds sway in modern Western society as much as it does anywhere else: we too have adolescents who wish to find out if they are pre-destined to achieve adulthood. These are youngsters who propitiate the goddess: so-called joy-riders, drug-takers and, in a more positive vein, backpackers who explore the remoter parts of the world – all of them are destiny-testers.

Many key principles follow on from this: a present-day rite of passage must also propitiate destiny. Its programme cannot be too anodyne; mishaps cannot be allowed to trigger compensation claims from participants, parents or guardians. Authorities can continue to prosecute programme organisers for avoidable negligence. Barring claims for compensation needn't mean lower standards of safety.

I have also considered a further interesting problem: change of status, and therefore in a sense rite of passage, can be achieved in a very passive and inactive way. The transition stage in rite of passage need not be characterised by programmes of derring-do or destiny testing. There's no need for any sort of programme at all! Martin Page (1972, p. 67) propounded the theory of ritual absence: simply making oneself incommunicado – this can be all that's necessary to induce change in social status. While incommunicado, mystical forces work their magic power: fiancés are converted into husband and wife; acerbic party politicians are converted into impartial governors-general.

The question now becomes: why propitiate capricious destiny when one can slope off for a quiet few weeks into the bush or onto the ocean? The answer is that if exiting childhood and entering adulthood were a simple matter of a few weeks absence ritual, we would indeed have a simple solution. The critical factor is age. For many adolescents, encountering destiny is absolutely necessary; destiny, for them is paramount. Those beyond adolescence for the most part know their destiny; marrying couples, for example, know that their marriage, their new life together – *is* their new destiny.

Part VII

The previous section discussed the pioneering work of Dr David Blumenkrantz in the United States. Blumenkrantz has single-handedly given flesh and bones to the idea of rite of passage in a contemporary modern setting. He is rightfully the father of modern rite of passage. Our emphases differ: Blumenkrantz is a community psychologist; for him, rite of passage re-invigorates the community. He takes the Ashanti proverb: 'it takes a whole village to raise a child', inverting it to 'it takes a whole child to raise a village'. Blumenkrantz would give equal authority to both statements. My emphasis here is on the child and a programme of rite of passage. Spin-off for the community as a whole, which there certainly should be, would be a 'bonus'. The analysis of Blumenkrantz's programme concluded:

1) The meaning of the word 'rite' in the phrase 'rite of passage' must be acknowledged and given due weight: 'rite' is not just a word to be uttered; rite is to be performed. Western man's ability to yield to ritual should not be doubted.

2) For credibility and authority, rite of passage must be all-embracing. Piecemeal rite of passage will not take root. This means that all children must be expected to participate. In a free society, non-participation would be an option; but all those who, for whatever reason, choose to opt out must be prepared to pay a social price for doing so.

3) Rite of passage must have authority to grant 'passage' – that is, passage from one social status to another. Without this power it has no authority; and therefore no purpose. Without 'passage', the term *'rite of passage'* is meaningless; its use a misnomer.

Then there was the question of law. Blumenkrantz's pioneering Rite of Passage Experience (ROPE) programme operates within the confines of existing American law. Pragmatically, he may well have decided to get a programme up and running. His programme has bestowed undoubted benefit on tens of thousands of American children. The programme, as we have noted, does not, and cannot, confer formal change of status on its participants. There is no legal framework within which it can do so. Blumenkrantz might have to wait years to see appropriate legislation enacted. It would be much better to get on with the job!

This proposal is prepared to bide its time. It starts from scratch and the recommendations for new social statuses will inevitably provoke legal change. Measures to restrict access to rights and privileges will also require legislative approval; the same applies to measures to curtail compensation claims arising from alleged negligence.

You should not imagine an operational rite-of-passage programme could be instituted tomorrow morning. This might be desirable but it's not realistic. This work sets an agenda that may take many years to realise. As the vision of this proposal for a present-day rite-of-passage programme unfolds, you will perceive that its implementation may require, in the United Kingdom, a new Act of Parliament. The same legislative imperative would apply to other jurisdictions – including the United States. The need, therefore, for legislative support is a principle predicating the launch of this and, in my view, any other viable rite-of-passage proposal.

There were further observations: Blumenkrantz noted the contrast that while the work of initiation is individual, responsibility for its transformative potential belongs to the community. Blumenkrantz also quoted Prof. Some who reminds us: 'a village is a village because it is held together by a shrine'. Every batch of youths, their mentors and families, will need a physical focal point at which progress in rite of passage can be checked and at which graduation can be celebrated. Blumenkrantz identified the actors in rite of passage: the adolescent, of course; his or her parent/s or guardian/s; mentors who may be community elders or recently graduated young adults, or both. These roles, particularly mentors, reflect traditional practice. Traditional practice recognises, controls and contains 'angry young man syndrome'. Mentors monitor and when necessary restrain their agitated charge.

Having reviewed the contents of the book so far I will now introduce my proposal for a present-day rite of passage that can be applied to Western societies.

30
SUGGESTION FOR A PRESENT-DAY RITE OF PASSAGE

SETTING THE SCENE

Life-skills, life-experience and mission-challenge: these are the three constituents of this suggestion for a present-day rite-of-passage programme. Each element is explained in outline in Chapter 32 and in greater detail in Chapter 33.

Meanwhile, the next two chapters are devoted to setting the scene. For before getting to the proposals in detail there are a number of prefatory questions to be asked, argued and decided upon. As is so often the case, one question leads to another. As, at this stage, the very concept of rite of passage is still theoretical, there must be a limit to how much can be asked and argued and deliberated upon.

Certain key questions are inescapable. Is rite of passage for *both* sexes? At what age should it begin? How long should it last? These questions underlie *any* rite of passage.

Other questions are intrinsic to the particular programme proposed here. How should this rite-of-passage programme be administered? Does this programme depend on any changes in law? If so, what changes?

This latter is dealt with first. That rite of passage should apply to *all* children and that a programme must be able to grant children passage from one defined status (child) to another defined status (adult) suggests, however, that these questions may be of general importance and not just intrinsic to the particular programme put forward here. The reader will no doubt quickly form his or her own opinion.

1 Politics

Inevitably, this proposal for a present-day rite of passage introduces contemporary political issues. Suffice to say, there has been no conscious attempt to promote any one political theory above another. What follows is not a blueprint for a present-day Hitler Youth. Hopefully, you will find the measures in this proposal a mixed bag, extending to all sides of the political spectrum. As for the Hitler Youth, its impact and its impression should not be underestimated. In his *Rise and Fall of the Third Reich* (1971, pp. 318–19) William L. Shirer wrote:

> In such a manner were the youth trained for life and work and death in the Third Reich. Though their minds were deliberately poisoned, their regular schooling interrupted, their homes largely replaced so far as their rearing went, the boys and the girls, the young men and women, seemed immensely happy, filled with the zest of life of a Hitler Youth. And there was no doubt that the practice of bringing the children of all classes and walks of life together, where those who had come from poverty or riches, from a labourer's home or a peasant's or a businessman's, or an aristocrat's, shared common tasks, was good and healthy in itself. In most cases it did no harm to a city boy and girl to spend six months in the compulsory Labour Service, where they lived outdoors and learned the value of getting along with those of different backgrounds. No one who travelled up and down Germany in those days and talked with the young in their camps and watched them work and play and sing could fail to see that, however sinister the teaching, here was an incredibly dynamic youth movement.
>
> The young in the Third Reich were growing up to have young and healthy bodies, faith in the future of their country and in themselves and a sense of fellowship and camaraderie that shattered all class and economic and social barriers. I thought of that later, in the May days of 1940, when along the road between Aachen and Brussels one saw the contrast between the German soldiers, bronzed and clean-cut from a youth spent in the sunshine on an adequate diet, and the first British war prisoners, with their hollow chests, round shoulders, pasty complexions and bad teeth – tragic examples of the youth that England had neglected so irresponsibly in the years between the wars.

Human behaviour, alas, is inconsistent; evil and genius are sometimes inextricably linked.

2 RITE OF PASSAGE: A ONE-SIZE-FITS-ALL SCHEME?

This short extract on the Hitler Youth introduces a difficult problem. Shirer writes of the minds of German Youth being 'deliberately poisoned'. German youth were encouraged to believe they were members of a super race. Excluded from their ranks were the children of those who were deemed *untermenschen* (subhuman): people with dark skin, gypsies, Jews and others. Nazi racism prevented their participation. Given the opportunity, many parents from these groups might have liked their children to take part.

But a problem arises: what should our attitude be to those groups who don't want their youth to take part in a one-size-fits-all state-organised programme? There will be some close-knit communities whose children are their treasure; who won't care what a rite-of-passage proposal contains, or what it doesn't; who will insist on educating and socialising their children in their own way and who will not accept unwelcome state intrusion. To compound the dilemma, these will be groups who rear their children extremely well. Their children never, or rarely, cause trouble in the public domain.

POSSIBLE DISSENTING GROUPS

Ultra-orthodox Jewish sects (Hasidim) are very self-contained and might be an example of a group which does not wish to take part in a one-size-fits-all state-organised programme. There may be more. The Amish people of New England in the United States are another sect who guard traditional values. The last thing one wants is for rite of passage to exacerbate the very problem it's designed to solve. As the old saying goes: 'If it ain't broke, don't fix it.' Rite of passage is designed to counteract adolescent misbehaviour. Why risk harming a community where this misbehaviour is not a problem?

There are unlikely to be many whole-communities to which this applies. Few whole-communities retain strict control of their teenage children. Adolescence, as a process, usually sees control weaken. Individual parents *start* in strict control of their children; few maintain such control through their children's teenage years. They might wish for such control, but they rarely have it.

The number of whole-communities maintaining hundred per cent control of their children's behaviour will be few and far between. There will, however, be plenty of groups whose membership comprises a 'broad church'. At the centre of the broad church may be members who are strictly orthodox, for example, members of religious groups: Christians, Muslims, Hindus and others; or, for example, members of secular groups, such as vegetarians. Some people within these groups will require rite of passage to be modified to their needs.

What is the resolution of this problem to be?

Every child must have the right *not* to take part in rite of passage – simply on grounds of personal disinclination. But it would be unethical for children, perhaps at their parents' behest, to have to invoke this right as an excuse for not taking part when the *real* reason was religious or cultural.

Groups who wish to do so must therefore be allowed to develop and administer rite of passage from their own base. The word *base* is used advisedly. This will be the residence in which children are based. At this residence, group orthodoxy – prayer, diet, dress, whatever – may be maintained.

What cannot be compromised is contact with the 'outside' world. Children from a restricted base cannot be shielded from the diversity that the outside world represents. The whole point of rite of passage is to engage in the process of socialisation, and to be able to savour the maturity that is its fruit.

This means that a rite-of-passage programme can cater to individual group needs but never to the extent that its fundamental integrity is breached. Perhaps the following suggestions might help:

a) Costs *extra* to those incurred by the state might be borne by any group wishing to maintain its own group base. The extra cost of special dietary requirements would be an example. Should a group wish their children to be together in their own group residence, they might then be expected to fund and provide the residence.

b) A child should give his or her written consent to participate in rite of passage on a group rather than state basis.

c) A one-size-fits-all scheme would be preferable. This would allow children of all backgrounds to socialise and mature together. This is a worthy aim. However, by conceding groups the right to keep children in their own group base, other important principles are being upheld; such principles include:

i) Acknowledging the overall responsibility of *parents* to raise their children. This includes parents urging their children into, and seeing their children through, rite of passage as they, the parents, see fit. Parents should be able to ensure that essential cultural values are not compromised by rite of passage.

ii) Parents themselves should accept that youth, properly matured, will behave maturely.

iii) The democratic principle should be upheld. Democracies are tested by the way they treat their minorities. Rite of passage can be no exception.

3 ADOLESCENT SELF-RESPECT AND PUBLIC RESPECT

It realty doesn't matter what a rite-of-passage programme entails; it will be effective as long as everybody eligible is expected to participate. In post-war Britain, National Service recruits complained about stultifying boot polishing and 'square-bashing'; but everybody did their stint. Youth crime figures began to rise dramatically when National Service was abolished in 1962. Although National Service did not formally deliver 'passage' in the sense we have been talking about, it seemed to do so informally. Many people felt, including recruits themselves, that youngsters had been transformed and matured by the experience.

In introducing rite of passage, the state will be saying to adolescents, perhaps for the first time: 'We (the state, society as a whole), know who you are; we know you're still formally a child; we know that we want you to leave childhood behind you and we know you want this too. Whenever you're ready, we're here to help you on the way. There's a right way a wrong way. We've set up a programme to enable you to do it in the right way, which is called 'rite of passage'. When you've completed this everyone will know that you've done so. All being well, you will be able to enter adulthood as a mature and confident young person. You will publicly be treated with respect and, just as importantly, you will be possessed of your own self-respect.'

The obvious criticism of this would be to label it 'Big Brother' or 'Nanny', the simple response to which would be to plead guilty! I believe that words to the above effect will be music to children's ears. It's exactly what they want to hear. Young people need this kind of help. It is help that can only come from the state.

Young people may be compared to motor vehicles: in the same way that motor vehicles are not allowed to career around our roads without formal (and regular) testing, so adolescents should not be allowed to 'career around society' without adequate preparation. To get onto the road in the first place, all motor vehicles must pass construction and use regulations. Adolescents should be no different. Rite of passage may be considered as the human equivalent of construction and use!

Recalling the Polish writer, Joseph Conrad, the philosopher Bertrand Russell writes in his book *Portraits from Memory* (1956, p. 82):

> He [Conrad] was very conscious of the various forms of passionate madness to which men are prone, and it was this that gave him such a profound belief in the importance of discipline. His point of view one might perhaps say, was the antithesis of Rousseau's: 'Man is born in chains, but he can become free'. He becomes free, so I believe Conrad would have said, not by letting loose his impulses, not by being casual and uncontrolled, but by subduing wayward impulse to a dominant purpose.

The words 'dominant purpose' may cause you to become apprehensive, but you should have no fear: the section on 'Vetting' (Chapter 36, below) is entirely devoted to safeguarding rite of passage from political input.

4 Law

Giving rite of passage legal status is one thing; but what precise changes in (UK) law are recommended? This particular proposal recommends two: a new law on status which will formalise child and adult status and introduce a new intermediary status; and an amendment to existing (UK) law on compensation claims.

Regarding the latter, it is proposed that: injury or death sustained in accidents arising from rite-of-passage activity will not be subject to claim for compensation for negligence. This would apply to claims by adolescents or their families. This echoes the ritual formula used by the Mende in cases of death in initiation ('I am sorry to tell you that the pot you have given me to fire is broken', Chapter 15, above). Every encouragement should be given to the idea that an adolescent participating in rite of passage is 'dicing with destiny', and to some extent this will be true. Rite of passage *will* be an engagement with destiny. This does not preclude programme providers maintaining, and being subjected by law to, the most stringent standards of safety regulation.

5 Is rite of passage for both sexes?

Adolescent female misbehaviour is a new, bewildering and escalating phenomenon. The number of Female Young Offender institutions in Britain has increased over the last three decades. In the United States, offences committed by female juveniles have increased considerably. Between 1989 and 1993, the growth-rate for female juvenile arrests was more than double the growth in arrests of males according to the 1996 Report of the US Office for Juvenile Justice and Delinquency Prevention.

The question is: is this behaviour copycatting adolescent male misbehaviour? Or, does it represent a unique class of its own? If female misbehaviour is 'copycat', then it would presumably abate if male misbehaviour declined. If, on the other hand, female misbehaviour is generic, female misbehaviour would continue after male misbehaviour has subsided. The question is worth deciding. Applying a rite-of-passage programme to females could be a duplication of resource and effort. Desirable as a rite of passage might be in its own right, it's surely expensive and pointless to deliver it gratuitously.

For males, rite of passage will be the vital social mechanism by which childhood is exited and adulthood entered. But, is exit and entrance really a problem for girls? We have already suggested: 'the menstrual cycle confirms, and every month re-confirms, the young female in her newly acquired womanhood. The young male has no comparative equivalent' (Chapter 11, above).

The menstrual cycle is a biological phenomenon, while education is an intellectual process. Neither, it can be argued, fulfils the essential social role of rite of passage. Males and females may be equally well educated but may nevertheless be equally immature. For this reason, we can argue, females should take part in the process of socialisation that is rite of passage. There is another reason too: hopefully, the rite-of-passage programme will be thought much too good to miss! Girls would find it unthinkable not to take part. There is, however, a 'but' ...

RITE OF PASSAGE MUST BE DIRECTED TO EACH SEX SEPARATELY.

There are three reasons why:

a) In Chapter 4 (above) reference was made to a private survey conducted in 1995 (see Appendix 1). The survey consisted of a number of propositions to which young people were asked to indicate assent or dissent. One proposition questioned:

> Males and females, **socially** speaking, mature into adults in **different** ways and by **different** processes? Disagree / Agree

to which 83% of boys and 92% of girls underlined 'agree'; 530 schoolchildren plus 104 young offenders were consulted.

If young people themselves believe the two sexes 'move along different paths' to mature separately, why should we not concur? A rite-of-passage programme administered separately would reflect this.

b) Young males need 'time out' from females, especially while seeking maturity. They need to discover themselves as males – to be by themselves and in male company. Rite of passage is the right time and place for this. Boys and girls, as has been suggested, mature at differing momentums. Allowance should be made for this.

c) In traditional societies, rite of passage is usually administered separately to each sex. This may reflect sexual role demarcation, which is not a factor in Western society where sexual equality and homogeneity are the norm. Nevertheless, I feel instinctively it would be wise to preserve the accumulated wisdom of centuries. Tradition should be respected and perpetuated.

6 WHEN MIGHT RITE OF PASSAGE BEGIN AND HOW LONG SHOULD IT LAST?

Change in terminology: Arnold van Gennep originated the phrase 'rite of passage' and detailed three stages: '(1) separation, (2) transitional period with gradual removal of barriers, (3) reintegration into ordinary life' (1960, p. 44). This classification is not cast in stone. I shall use different terms which reconnect with our introductory theme: Shakespeare's monologue 'All the world's a stage' in which 'players' have 'their exits and their entrances'.

Van Gennep's first stage of 'separation' is changed to 'exit-age'. 'Exit' therefore refers to formal departure from childhood. 'Entrance-age' or just 'entrance' refers to van Gennep's final stage: 'reintegration into ordinary life'. Finally, 'passage-time' replaces van Gennep's 'transitional period'. 'Time' gives the idea of duration, how long a rite of passage lasts; and 'passage' reinforces the word 'passage' in the phrase *rite of passage*: bringing to mind helpful associations of time spent 'in passage', being 'outside in a passage', and 'working one's passage'.

Incidentally, van Gennep would, I feel, have approved of Shakespeare's lines to introduce his beliefs. Van Gennep wrote: 'The life of an individual in any society is a series of passages from one age to another and from one occupation to another' (1966, p. 2). Shakespeare, as we have seen, foretold this a little more poetically substituting 'age' for 'stage' .

Exit-age

When should rite of passage begin? When should children first exit childhood and the process of shedding childhood status first start? These questions assume that children wish to exit childhood as soon as they can. For many, this will indeed be the case. In traditional societies, the urge is strong to lose childhood status as soon as possible (Saitoti 1980 tell us, for instance, how Maasai boys and girls spend hours checking whether their pubic hair has grown). Children in Western society may be similarly motivated.

In theoretical terms, rite of passage may be initiated at any time. Common sense is the only imperative. Van Gennep observed that physical and what he styled social puberty rarely coincide. There is therefore no need to co-ordinate the two. In any case, the onset of physical puberty varies from child to child. This proposal allows for entry into rite of passage either during school or after school.

An after-school rite-of-passage programme may be delivered as one sustained course; while a during-school rite of passage, concurrent and competing with school education will inevitably take longer to administer. During-school rite of passage is not ideal. Education and socialisation (rite of passage) are of equivalent status. They should not, however, be confused; nor should they be made to compete with one another. As the saying goes, 'business' (education) 'should not be mixed with pleasure' (socialisation). The serious school student will wish to use evenings, weekends and holidays for study for exams. There is no good reason why he or she should be penalised at the expense of non-academic pupils who regard these times as free. It may be that an accommodation can be made, although at this theoretical stage it's not quite clear exactly what that accommodation might be.

The case in favour of during-school rite of passage involves youth crime figures. These suggest that antisocial adolescent misbehaviour peaks at the relatively early ages of 15–17. Insofar as our basic theory informs that this misbehaviour derives from fundamental frustration at being unable to shed childhood status, it follows that the earlier the remedy (rite of passage) is started, the better. In this context, this proposal for a present-day rite of passage allows for a child to first enrol on the day of his or her *14th* birthday.

After-school entry can be at any time. It allows children to complete their school education before addressing rite of passage; it allows for children who, for whatever reason, do not wish to enter rite of passage until their late teens or twenties. No child will be compelled to participate in rite of passage. For those who don't wish to undertake rite of passage, full adult status would be granted automatically at the age of 30 or 35.

Formal 'exit' from childhood is a brief event. It's a moment to say goodbye: a verbal (if temporary) goodbye to parents and loved ones; a literal goodbye to childhood. It's a moment to be savoured in drama and symbolism; definitely a time for the 'rite' in rite of passage to be celebrated.

ENTRANCE INTO ADULTHOOD

Entrance into adulthood may similarly be a brief event; but, then again, it may not! Recalling van Gennep's description of passage-time (he used the term 'transitional period') 'with gradual removal of barriers', the gradual removal of barriers could be made to mean gradual bestowal of privilege. Adult privileges – the right to vote, drive, inherit and other rights – can all either be awarded together or be drip-fed in stages. A privilege, or series of privileges, can be bestowed as each sub-stage of passage-time is completed. Once again, at this theoretical stage, everything is open to suggestion: these are ideas, which may be adopted or not, as seen fit.

Adolescents should mark entitlement to new rights and privileges by ritual celebration which can be formal, informal or both. Any and every opportunity to party should be taken.

PASSAGE-TIME: HOW LONG SHOULD IT LAST?

Passage-time obviously will occupy the lion's share of time spent in rite of passage. There are two separate considerations: first, the time the rite-of-passage programme takes to deliver; secondly, who decides, and how, that a candidate is fit to graduate.

First, how long it takes to deliver the rite-of-passage programme obviously depends on the content of the programme. Our proposal divides into life-experience and mission. Life-experience further subdivides. To quantify how long the programme will last is impossible at this stage. Everything always takes longer than anticipated.

Blumenkrantz's contemporary Rite of Passage Experience (Part VII, Chapters 25–8, above), for example, is conceived and delivered as a three-phase six-year programme. I would not wish my programme to last as long as this as candidates might lose heart. Ideally, I would like to see the during-school programme last three years, from 14 to 17. Possibly a further six months could be added for a child to complete the intended mission-challenge stage of rite of passage. The after-school version might last a year or 18 months.

Secondly, regarding the question of who decides a candidate is fit to graduate, my answer is that nobody decides: anyone who puts in the time is automatically fit. Rite of passage is not an intellectual exam-taking process and may it never be so! Rite of passage is a socialising process where experience reigns supreme. He or she who has savoured the experience has successfully undertaken rite of passage. The only measure to be recorded is a candidate's presence and engagement in experience when offered the opportunity to participate.

31
THREE SOCIAL STATUSES

FROM CHILD TO ADULT VIA SOCIAL CHILD

This proposal for a present-day rite of passage is designed to accomplish a formal transformation in social status. No such transformation can be achieved until the social statuses in question have been acknowledged and formalised.

This plan takes account of children who for reasons of conscientious objection, or whatever, do not wish to participate in rite of passage. Nevertheless, these children must be accorded status in the scheme of things. They will bear a status which makes their as yet non-participation in rite of passage explicit, something which everybody will be aware of.

In this proposal, there are therefore *three* stages of social status. It is important to understand that before a particular social status can be publicly discarded, it must be up and running so-to-speak and in the public eye. The three stages are:

1) *Child*: as currently understood, this stage applies until his or her 14th birthday.

2) *Social child*: the formal social status to be given to young people between the ages of 14 and 30 or 35 (at which age it has been suggested full adult status may be bestowed automatically); social child will therefore be the status of all those who have, for whatever reason, chosen not to convert themselves into adults by embarking on rite of passage. It will also be the formal status of young people whilst they are engaged in rite of passage but have not yet graduated.

3) *Adult*: the social status acquired automatically at the age of 30 or 35, but possibly as early as 17/18 on fulfilment of rite of passage.

TITLE AND SOCIAL STATUS

Orthographically, title and social status can be signified fairly simply.

Child status will be signified by not prefacing a name with a title, e.g.

- John Smith
- Mary Jones

In the relatively rare event of a child bearing a title, then the status of child must be made explicit, e.g.

- The Hon. John Smith (child)
- Lady Mary Jones (child)
- Prince John (child)
- Princess Catherine (child)

Social child status will be signified by prefacing the name with a title whose first letter will always be printed in lower case, e.g.

- mr John Smith;
- miss, ms or mrs Mary Jones

Once again, titles can be signified but in lower case, e.g.

- sir John Smith
- lady Mary Jones
- prince John
- princess Catherine

Adult status will be signified as is currently the case, e.g.

- Mr John Smith
- Miss, Ms or Mrs Mary Jones
- Sir John Smith
- Lady Mary Jones
- Prince John
- Princess Catherine

Every state-originated communication will observe these conventions. This will include schools and universities. Every employer will wish to do so too. Orally, every youngster should reckon on being asked: 'Mister Smith? Big "M" or little "m"?'

So from a 'passage' point of view, the rite of passage from child to adult is the passage from 'Smith' to 'Mr Smith' via, for a period of time, at each youngster's own discretion, 'mr' Smith. The same applies for females, every single member of society in fact – princes and princesses included.

Comment on each status

1 General

Emphasising personal social status reflects conclusions arrived at from examining the Japanese experience (Part V, The Japanese Way, Chapters 17–19). To requote from the review of Part V (Chapter 29, above):

> This phenomenon in Japanese language and culture [(extreme concentration on personal status] confirms the fundamental speculation of this work: adolescent misbehaviour and ambiguity in social status are inextricably linked. Create certainty, eliminate ambiguity, and delinquency will recede of its own accord.

A youngster wishing to shed childhood status can now best do so by engaging as soon as practicable in rite of passage. The existing option – embarking upon an ad hoc programme of adolescent misbehaviour – will be purposeless. The tactic, once logical, now has no point. The old gallery of ego, peer group and older generation are still around and they are still spectators; but they have progressed from 'street' theatre. They're all now established critics at the new 'life-school' theatre of rite of passage.

There will be further incentive to opt for rite of passage. Completion of rite of passage confers earlier access to life's privileges, hitherto denied. More about this later.

2 Comment on child

There's a difference between naughtiness and delinquency. All children are naughty at times; not all however are delinquent. The distinction must to some extent be arbitrary. Three factors escalate naughtiness into delinquency: (a) misbehaviour outside the family environment; (b) sustaining such misbehaviour; and (c) misbehaviour causing, or intended to cause, damage to property or person.

The question is how to control a juvenile delinquent as young as eight or ten? The child's delinquency may be caused by serious psychological disorder. The reason may be known; the resultant behaviour is no less difficult to control. However, delinquency may be driven by no more than a young child's desire prematurely to exit childhood. In this latter case, it's possible to suggest a response. One possible response would be to defer the age at which the child would first be able to start rite of passage to later than 14. Delay would be a heavy penalty; perhaps one to be imposed by a child court or similar institution. The danger of course is that a delay might exacerbate the problem.

Waiting until 14 to start rite of passage may be too long for some children. One hopes that knowledge of rite of passage's impending approach will tame delinquent tendencies. For some children, this hope may be in vain. We may still have to learn how to control the phenomenon of 'prepubescent' delinquency.

CHILD AND SOCIAL CHILD: SUSPENSION OF RIGHTS AND PRIVILEGES

Currently, in the United Kingdom, as elsewhere in Western society, a child becomes entitled to rights and privileges at varying ages. By rights and privileges, we mean the trappings of adulthood: provisional driving licence (17); age of legal majority including the right to inherit and own property (18).

It is a key measure in *this* particular proposal for a present-day rite of passage that access to the trappings of adulthood is to be denied. Access will become possible only after a (social) child enters adulthood. This will be either on completion of rite of passage or at automatic entrance (at age 30 or 35). Not before.

It may be that a particular trapping of adulthood, for example the right to learn to drive, can be 'drip-fed' as part of a rite-of-passage experience. A provisional licence could be granted during rite of passage. This could be converted to a full licence on completion, but rescinded if completion isn't fulfilled.

There is one entitlement that cannot be denied, namely the right to marry. This is currently conceded at the age of 16 (in the UK) provided both parties have written parental consent. Marriage at this early age is rare, but sex among young people of this age is not! The sexual imperative runs deeper than rite of passage! This just has to be accepted.

A girl giving birth prior to rite of passage may condemn herself to 'social-childhood' status – with all its disadvantages – for a long time. How much of a disincentive this will be only time will tell.

3 COMMENT ON 'SOCIAL CHILD'

The concept of 'social child' is fundamental to this proposal. Social child will be a new and formal status. The term 'social child' is certainly intended to be a codeword for 'immature adult' or 'unsocialised adult'.

My idea for social child derives from the field experience of students of human culture. In this context, the reader is reminded of La Fontaine's report (1985, p. 103) cited previously (p.56) that Gisu men, however old they might be, were not entitled to drink beer with other men unless they had been initiated. Uninitiated men who somehow or other slipped through the net would be contemptuously referred to as 'boys' even if married with children.

A similar attitude was noted towards girls among the Bemba people, neighbours of the Gisu, who referred to uninitiated girls as 'rubbish'. The underlying point is that among tribal peoples who traditionally require rite of passage to mark maturity, the identity of initiates is a matter of public knowledge. The names of those who avoid rite of passage are generally known and these people are often looked down upon.

This proposal's lower-case upper-case letter system (as set out above) for titling individuals will make social status a matter of instantly ascertainable public knowledge. 'Despising' those who, for whatever reason, elect not to participate in rite of passage, is unworthy and unnecessary. Nevertheless there will be stigma. 'Social child' will be a limbo period; a social status without access to privilege; a social status to occupy for as short a time as possible.

At the end of the day one cannot have it both ways. Rite of passage must have 'teeth'. Voluntary programmes have no social force whatsoever. The dice are therefore loaded in favour of participating in rite of passage; and the dice are equivalently loaded against non-participation.

Finally, one has to ask what is so wrong in wishing maturity upon youth. This is a reasonable wish, born out of consideration for the well being of each and every young person and nothing to be ashamed of. Able-bodied young people who deny themselves the experience of rite of passage must surely be regarded for what they are – adult in age but social children in all other respects.

4 Comment on adult status

Successfully managed transition of child to adult will generate a rich reward: society will be provided with a nucleus of mature youth, sure of its place in the world and confident in its ability to fill that place. Traditional society bears witness to this. As Saitoti (1980, p. 124) writes:

> To become a warrior is the dream of every Maasai youth; the world itself seems to convey magical powers. A warrior must be strong, clever, courageous, confident, wise and gentle ... In addition to the practical services they provide for the group they live among, warriors also add an immeasurable sense of excitement, adventure and romance; without their songs,

> their poetry, their flirting, their bold masculinity, Maasai life would not be the same.

There are few roles for warrior as such in societies of high technology. What a pity! Warrior is precisely the role sought by today's young. So many are macho wannabes ineffectually attempting to enter an adult world. In a piece entitled, 'Inside the Mind of a Graffiti Lout' (*Daily Mail*, 11 September 1989), a hooligan, who on his latest spree had caused £30,000 worth of clean-up damage to (then) British Rail, was quoted as saying:

> spraying those carriages gave me a feeling of danger. A bit like the war, I reckon. The more dangerous it is, the more respect you get from other graffiti writers. BR [British Rail] weren't going to be happy, but we didn't care. They can afford it anyway.

The hooligan has a point. As Churchill wrote: 'Existence is never so sweet than when it is at hazard.'

The big trick then is for the establishment to take over: for the establishment to provide 'warrior-opportunities' to all those that want them. In the passage and progress along 'destiny's corridor', there will be young people who will consciously opt to challenge destiny; there will also be those whom destiny will haphazardly challenge of her own accord.

Our rite-of-passage proposal will give ample opportunity for individuals to discover themselves, for their personality and character to be revealed to the world and to themselves. Destiny awaits.

32
A Present-day Rite of Passage

Suggestions in Outline

The Power of Ritual Drama: Overnight Transformation

The reader may recall the story, recounted by La Fontaine, and cited earlier in Chapter 9. This was about the two men from the Herero people among whom Prof. La Fontaine was conducting fieldwork. As boys, they told her, they had had a playmate, a young girl of their own age. She had suddenly been whisked off to undergo initiation. When she returned she was completely oblivious of her previous friends. The two men looked to La Fontaine for a satisfactory explanation for what seemed to them extraordinary behaviour. Perhaps, they thought, that La Fontaine, as a woman, would validate their suspicion – that this is the way girls behave. What La Fontaine told them, we do not know. But this is what she says to *us*:

> The ritual experience changed her: she had become a woman and they were still little boys.
>
> La Fontaine, 1985, p. 185

We are not told precisely how long the girl was away. But it is unlikely to have been for very long. Perhaps a month, at the most.

So the question inevitably raises itself: what are we doing proposing a rite-of-passage programme lasting a year when the job can perhaps be done in a month or two or even less.

There are two responses to this question.

The first is this: perhaps rite of passage *can* be delivered in the short period of a month or two. What a bonus! What a huge saving in cost! What a simple answer to the blight of young human life, ravaged, we believe, by the lack of rite of passage. If the formula advanced earlier (Chapter 12) – absence ⇨ secrecy ⇨ mystique = background conditions for effecting change of social status – is correct, why should it only work in highly ritualised societies? It could work for our society too.

I am not a psychologist. I have hitherto resisted attempting to analyse the underlying causes of the mystical and transformational power of ritual. But it may be something as simple as 'expectation': self-expectation, peer group expectation and adult/older-generation expectation. If ritual drama instils the idea that people are *expected* to behave in a certain way, then maybe this is all we have to do.

The young Herero girl mentioned above conducted herself after her rite of passage the way she and all her peer group were expected to. Similarly, the Japanese interact in accordance with strict social expectation; British Members of Parliament too.

But we are not Japanese. Neither are we members, unlike the Herero and the Maasai and other tribal peoples, of what some students of human culture have called 'small-scale' societies. Therein lies the second response: that there is so much to learn about the grand scale of our own society that, even utilising to our advantage the power of ritual to effect transformation, each social child still needs a year (or more) to learn about him- or herself and the wider world in which he or she lives.

In the breadth of modern society, maturity is more than a matter of bearing and behaviour. Though, whilst surveying the disarray of contemporary youth, many people might be quite prepared to settle for as little as this.

A PRESENT-DAY RITE OF PASSAGE

1 LIFE-SKILLS

A first step to maturity must be the ability to look after oneself indoors and outdoors. To this end, we conceive an initial series of courses devoted to instilling self-reliance. Courses would be basic. Each might last no more than a week. On completion each (social-) child might receive a certificate of accomplishment. This *could* indicate the degree of proficiency achieved. The only caveat is to remember that rite of passage is not school or university. It is not to be examination based. If and when Destiny intrudes, she will test character not technique. It cannot be denied, though, that the two are inextricably linked. In an extreme moment, proficiency and technique learned from a life-skill course, or courses, could easily turn out to be the saving grace.

PROPOSED LIFE-SKILL COURSES

Courses are merely listed here. Each will be discussed in more detail in the next chapter.

a) *Indoor domesticities*

   i) Hygiene – how to use a washing machine, spin-dryer; how to iron; how to clean, to sew and to mend

   ii) Cooking – how to boil, fry and bake

   iii) Home Economics – how to budget and to shop

b) *Indoor and outdoor*

   i) First Aid – learning what to do, and, just as important, what **not** to do in an accident or an emergency

c) *Outdoor*

   i) Orienteering – how to read an Ordnance Survey map and how to read a compass

   ii) A week's cross-country hike

   iii) Dangerous sports – land: rock and mountain climbing, abseiling; water/sea: swimming and diving; sailing

   iv) Two candidate-choice life-skills from a selection

2 LIFE-EXPERIENCE: A 'TOUR AROUND SOCIETY'

ENCOUNTER, WITNESS AND SAMPLE

Rite-of-passage candidates might be sent on what can be called 'a tour around society'.

I call this 'tour' life-experience.

Life-experience will be particularly important for candidates whose world-view has been confined to the locale in which they have been born and bred: young people who, for whatever reason, are unlikely to have left their home ground. Many young people are in this predicament. Life-experience is an opportunity to gain awareness of the variety of occupations in the modern world; and in gaining this awareness, it is also an opportunity for the candidate to widen his or her own horizons. Whilst rite of passage is not intended to be in any way vocational, a chance contact here or there may create awareness of career possibilities in areas totally new to a candidate's experience.

The process of encountering, witnessing and wherever possible sampling the everyday working lives of other people is designed to help the average rite-of-passage candidate to mature. This is the hope. For the vast majority of candidates, the overview of society that life-experience will offer will be a once-in-a-lifetime occurrence.

Not every candidate will be seconded to an army unit, jump from a plane, dive from a boat or ride in an ambulance, fire-engine or police car; many will experience less glamorous attachments – to a school, to a library, a court or a prison. With luck, every candidate could receive an interesting mix of attachments.

The intention is that each candidate will understand that he or she is a part of a wider society; that society is ultimately an integrated entity; and that inevitably, in a sophisticated industrial society, it is the lot of each individual – except in rare cases – to occupy the role of a tiny cog in one small part of a wheel which is itself a wheel within a larger wheel. Unless one is royalty or prime minister, one will be unlikely to receive an overview of society as good as that given in rite of passage.

3 MISSION-CHALLENGE

Mission-challenge is the final part of the rite-of-passage programme. The word 'programme' is emphasised, as the culmination of rite of passage itself must be a well-organised, well-orchestrated graduation ceremony of considerable ritual drama. This should be held 'back in the village' from whence the whole process started.

Nearly half of the time of the rite-of-passage programme might be taken up in mission-challenge, some twenty weeks or so.

Mission-challenge is the posting of the rite-of-passage candidate to any position where he or she can be of service. Mission-challenge is community service. Foreign government agencies, national or local government agencies, and charities might all avail themselves of mission-challenge volunteers. Consequently, volunteers could find themselves almost anywhere: in a city or in the country; at home or abroad; in a first- or third-world setting.

More will be written about mission-challenge later. Suffice to say at this stage, that every candidate should be given the opportunity to practise at least some of the life- skills he or she has attained. They may be put to use in the service of the young or the elderly, a group or an individual. Hopefully, when called upon to perform, our young will not be at a loss.

IN SUMMARY

In summary a rite-of-passage programme might pan out as follows:

Life-skills acquisition period:

1.	Admission to rite of passage and first indoor domesticity course: Hygiene	1 week
2.	Cooking	1 week
3.	Home Economics	1 week
4.	First Aid	1 week
5.	Intervening life-experience course detailed in Chapter 34	2 week
6.	Orienteering	1 week
7.	Cross-country hike	1 week
8.	Dangerous sports: land	1 week
9.	Dangerous sports: water/sea	1 week
10.	Candidate's choice or air	1 week
	subtotal	*11 weeks*

Life-experience period:

11.	Nine randomly selected by computer plus one mandatory that all candidates attend	20 weeks
12.	Mission-challenge	20 weeks
	total	***51 weeks***

33
A Present-day Rite of Passage

Suggestions In Detail – Life-skills

Ability to read and write

Much has been made about rite of passage being a process of socialisation as opposed to education. There is however one educational requirement which I would suggest as a minimum benchmark for admission into rite of passage: this is the ability to read and write. Each candidate should be pre-tested on this.

In a rite-of-passage programme, there is bound to be written information to be absorbed. For reasons of safety, if nothing else, candidates must be able to understand what they are required to do, or *not* to do...

It is of course incredible that children can spend years at school without acquiring the basic ability to read and write. Knowledge that they will be tested in this before being allowed to embark on rite of passage could act as an incentive. Children might henceforth regard reading and writing as the one skill they *must* not fail to acquire.

Life-skill courses

The reader should remember that we are dealing in speculation. The proposed courses are suggestions. They may never materialise. Or, if they do, they may do so in an entirely different form. Therefore it is unwise to expend time going into too much detail. However, in principle, it would be a good idea if responsibility could circulate from candidate to candidate within the group. That said, we can have no idea what size a group will be.

As far as the first life-skill, hygiene, is concerned, candidates could practise what they are taught almost immediately: how to use washing machines, how to iron, wash, sew and mend.

The goal is self-reliance. With just these abilities plus input from the next life-skill, the candidate will have made a good start.

Cooking, budgeting and shopping

The cooking course is bound to be basic: how to boil, fry and bake. One cannot expect to absorb in a week a subject that is taught in colleges for a period of a year or more.

Of equal importance is training in cooking safety. A candidate may have to cook in the field. Training in the use of portable cooking equipment is therefore important. Failure to take proper precautions can lead to serious burns.

The course might also include advice on food preparation and kitchen hygiene. Learning to cook has a serious purpose, but it also could be a lot of fun. Candidates who enjoy cooking should be indulged: cakes, birthday treats, ethnic dishes of every kind should all be encouraged.

Budgeting and shopping (suggested third life-skill) inform all aspects of the first two life-skills. It is a good idea to know what things cost. In later life, many families break down from what seems, in retrospect, to have been little more than a failure to manage domestic money matters. An early grounding can do no harm. Shopping is a skill to be acquired, particular within a tight budget.

Fourth life-skill: first aid

Rite-of-passage candidates should learn first aid. Living in a society whose citizenry has been trained in first aid would be reassuring for everybody. Knowledge of what to do in accidents – what *not* to do, even – must be a valuable asset. As more and more young people fulfil rite of passage and graduate, first-aid capability would become near universal. This can only be for the good.

Once again, people might complain that a week is not enough. This is true. But a week's worth of knowledge in what is after all only *first* aid is better than none at all.

Fifth skill: map reading (orienteering) and a week's hiking and camping

Self-reliance may lead to leadership. The ability to negotiate 'the outdoors' might be a test of both. Reading an Ordnance Survey Map, following a compass and acquiring knowledge of appropriate clothing and precautionary techniques are all part of this vital experience.

Theory, I hope, can be translated into reality. Every candidate might sample the outdoors. A hike of perhaps a week's duration would be a memorable experience. The adventure might also prove an opportunity for candidates to alternate duties and responsibilities. Charge might pass from one candidate to another on a role-by-role basis, day-by-day or even hour-by-hour.

Leadership need not be on a strictly individual basis. Candidates might be grouped together in small teams. Responsibility might be discharged on a team basis.

One imagines that in the background, if not ostensibly, the adventure would be master-minded by adult and experienced leadership. This leadership might order the route, assess the terrain and call off the enterprise at the prospect or onset of adverse weather conditions.

Whilst I am all in favour of exposing candidates to the vagaries of capricious Destiny, there is no need to provoke Destiny irresponsibly and unnecessarily. Highest standards of safety should always prevail. The reader should remember that, in this proposal as imagined, for organisations that deliver, or *mis*-deliver, rite-of-passage programmes, prosecution for culpable negligence is a very real possibility. *Not* advocated, in this proposal as imagined, is any form of compensation at all for the victim or family of a candidate injured by accident, howsoever caused.

DANGEROUS SPORTS – LAND: ROCK AND MOUNTAIN CLIMBING; ABSEILING

Common sense must be allowed to prevail. Even in the tender teenage years, some children are physically challenged. Other children are temperamentally unsuited to danger. They could become a risk to themselves and/or to others. A hike over predominantly flat terrain is one thing; mountain and rock climbing quite another.

For candidates for whom, subjectively and/or objectively, mountain climbing and the like would be obviously unsuitable, it would be kinder to provide alternative life-skill courses.

One hopes that candidates would be allowed to opt out only as a last resort.

DANGEROUS SPORTS – WATER/SEA: SWIMMING, LIFE-SAVING; BOATING AND SAILING

This is an opportunity for each candidate to enhance his or her current abilities. For the candidate who cannot swim, this is a further week's (or maybe more) opportunity to learn. For the candidate who can swim, this skill might be upgraded by being taught life-saving techniques.

Be it on lake or open-sea, candidates should have the thrill of manoeuvring a boat – whether with paddles, oars or sail.

DANGEROUS SPORTS: AIR

Certain 'escapades' seem more dangerous than they really are. Having said this, one does hear of accidents from time to time. Two that come to mind are bungee and parachute jumping. Neither are life-skills though. They are however exciting and unforgettable experiences. Parachute jumping is available to the public. The participant jumps together with, and is secured to, an experienced exponent of parachuting.

Unless there are common-sense reasons why not, such as cost, perhaps rite-of-passage candidates might savour the excitement of a parachute jump. Bungee jumping and all other forms of 'air' experience can be ignored. For unlike land, and to a lesser extent sea, mastery of a skill in the air is not remotely vital to the average person.

CONCLUDING CONCERN

The reader might be able to think of many more life-skill courses from which candidates might benefit.

How might a candidate select from skill-courses available? Might the candidate opt for a course of quasi-apprenticeship? Does it matter if he or she does? Is rite of passage to be no more than a proxy for apprenticeship?

First of all, one is hardly likely to receive much of an apprenticeship in a period of just a few weeks. This is all the time allocated to life-skills of a candidate's choice. But the final part of rite of passage is mission-challenge. This lasts as long as twenty weeks. Mission-challenge is regarded as community service. Whether community service and personal apprenticeship *can* be blended is an interesting question. Whether they *should* be is another.

Considering we are discussing something that may not even get off the ground we can perhaps leave the matter open. My own view is that the two, community service and apprenticeship, are unlikely to be compatible. This is particularly the case when plans for 'rite-of-passage international' (see Chapter 35) are put forward.

34
A Present-day Rite of Passage

Suggestions in Detail – Life-experience

Encounter, witness and sample

The concept of life-experience has already been introduced. It has been described as a 'tour around society'. The watchwords are: encounter, witness and sample.

Life-experience has numerous objectives: to aid maturity; to receive an overview and gain knowledge of society as a whole; and to understand that except in very rare cases, life is lived out inevitably in a tiny cog within society's big wheel.

This tour around society emulates traditional experience. Maasai initiates, it will be recalled, wander through Maasailand entertained, feted and fed, from village to village.

Destiny (chance)

The reader will be aware that there has been an obsession with destiny – an aspect of which might be called chance. In this context, I would hope that candidate assignments to life-experience events and courses could be computer generated – on the assumption that there would be an almost infinite range of possibilities from which to choose. Candidates' exposure to particular life-experience programmes would thus be entirely a matter of chance.

Some life-experiences might be regarded as exciting; others boring. Accompanying police on patrol (if it can be arranged) might be more desirable than attachment to a library; time in a military unit more agreeable than attachment to a sewage farm; and so on. But one can never account for the vagaries of human nature; one man's meat is another man's poison. Hopefully, the computer will generate a varied assortment.

ALL THE WORLD'S A STAGE...

In this scheme as envisaged, participating units would offer candidates some sort of active role if at all possible. Participating units might be drawn from government, local government, private institutions, companies and the arts: i.e. everywhere.

AND MEET AND GREET THE BOSSES

As candidates complete (life-skill) course after course and (life) experience after experience, they might receive a certificate to mark each accomplishment. It would be a very good idea if certificates could be presented, and personally signed, by as many top personnel and organisational heads as can make themselves available for an award-giving rite-of-passage ceremony followed by a party.

Firstly, it would be good for candidates to encounter very senior personnel and meet them personally, however briefly. Secondly, it would be good for the very senior personnel themselves. 'It takes a whole village', says the West African proverb, 'to raise a child'. As senior members 'of the village', senior personnel, together with their subordinates, will legitimately be able to feel that they have played their part towards maturing the younger generation, rite-of-passage candidates.

Rite-of-passage candidates may come to regard the signed certificates as treasured mementoes. They might also cherish official photographs on which they appear with important and/or well known (public) figures.

THREE COMPULSORY LIFE-EXPERIENCES

1 – ENCOUNTER WITH DYING AND DEATH

Whether the term *life*-experience is apt in this context is open to question: but rite-of-passage candidates should spend time at a hospice; and then with an undertaker.

The reasoning behind this is to do with the way dying and death have been treated as taboos in Western society throughout the latter part of the twentieth and the early twenty-first century. Dying and death have been swept under the carpet. The taboo must now be removed. There are two reasons why.

Firstly, to restore 'balance' to life. The contention is this: yes, the process of dying, and its consequence, death, is always unpleasant. It would be better if it never happened. But it does – day in and day out. And creating a taboo out of dying and death is counter-productive. It does no-one any favours. By masking death, young people are deprived of knowledge and awareness of this essential counter-balance to life.

As a result, young people frequently begin leading their lives on the false premise that they must be happy all the time; and that if they're not, there's something deeply wrong. The plastic world of film and television advertising has elevated happiness into something that is not only portrayed as permanently achievable but also almost obligatory.

The sooner life is set into balance for young rite-of-passage candidates, the better. A period at a hospice would help establish this equilibrium. The stay would help to contextualise the world. Materialism may be placed in its proper perspective – an indispensable aid to happiness, but never its source. The source is love from human relationships. There is no better place to witness this than at a hospice.

So an early encounter with sadness and pain, maybe and paradoxically an encounter mixed with real joy, will enable young people to face life with balance and maturity.

The second reason highlights the role of destiny in human life. Time spent at a hospice will inevitably risk encountering those, children even, whose life destiny has decreed will shortly be coming to a premature end. Destiny, common to all faiths and creeds, we hold to be the guiding spirit behind rite of passage. In hospitals, hospices and nursing homes, candidates would observe in stark reality destiny's universal caprice. Candidates may well think: '*There but for the grace of destiny go I*' and '*What has destiny got in store for me?*'

If the experience of this encounter is harrowing, humbling and emotional, so be it. There's no shame. Help, by way of group discussion, counselling even, is always available. Also, rite of passage is fast moving and the candidate will soon move on. There should be little time to brood.

In a putative order of programme for rite of passage, I foresee this life-experience inserted very early on – perhaps immediately after first-aid and immediately before map-reading. Hopefully a candidate's young mind will soon be concentrating upon reading his or her Ordnance Survey map, not getting lost in the middle of a forest.

Encounter with dying and death is a, or even *the*, most important element in rite of passage. Every candidate should undergo this experience. The experience can be expected to be as life-enhancing as it is traumatic and vice-versa.

2 – WORKING WITH ANIMALS

For many candidates, working with or near animals will be a new experience. It will also be an opportunity to bear important responsibility.

Under supervision and with training, candidates may learn to care for a single animal or group of animals.

Feeding, cleaning and general welfare are all duties with which candidates might be entrusted. For howsoever short a period, one wants a candidate to experience a period when he or she was able to say: 'That animal or those animals have been relying on *me*' – or, if it's a group of candidates, '*us*'.

If a candidate is afraid of animals, there must be many things a candidate can do near animals without being in actual contact with them. Candidates might be attached to a farm or a veterinary surgery. For urban-dwelling candidates, the farm and its routines will be a new world – no bad thing for city or suburban youngsters to experience.

3 – Visiting seats of government

If one is going to spend the rest of one's life as a tiny cog within society's big wheel, it is reasonable on rite of passage to visit and spend time with those who make, or think they make, the big wheels (there are many) go round.

If one is a citizen of the United Kingdom, there would be lots of places to visit: the European Community centre at Brussels; The Houses of Parliament (Commons and Lords) and last, but not least, the seat of Local Authority government.

Other nations will have their equivalents. All are centres of history with whose institutions rite-of-passage candidates should become familiar.

Boring speeches... (it could be worse)

In addressing candidates, one hopes that politicians will be able to restrain themselves. Elders and betters sometimes have a tendency to sermonise. Candidates should just be grateful that they are not, in this instance at least, young Maasai warriors. These latter are obliged to endure hectoring harangues from their elders lasting many hours. Youth of course frequently fail to realise that over the years they too will inevitably glide into elderhood with its own set of cares and fears.

Concluding remarks

We finish where we began. It may be that a short absence (ritual) can deliver the mindset which motivates maturity and mature behaviour. If this is so, we *should* know about it. Inculcating our young with mature behaviour and a mature outlook is certainly the primary goal. But maturity in a relative vacuum is not enough. It must be balanced against a wider awareness. This wider awareness is needed to live and function in the technologically advanced societies of the West. In this scenario, rite-of-passage kick-start life-experiences are a prerequisite for maturity.

35
Mission-Challenge and International Rite of Passage

Mission-Challenge – A Problem Yet to be Resolved

In this particular suggestion for a rite-of-passage programme, the third and final element has been called mission-challenge It occupies the lion's share of the year-long period proposed – some twenty weeks.

The first point to make is this: if there is to be 'during-school' rite of passage, this feature cannot be administered. Life-skill and life-experience events, yes; but not mission-challenge. An interlude of twenty weeks is impossible to find within the confines of a school curriculum. Perhaps this mission-challenge element could be suspended to wait for formal schooling to be concluded.

This suggestion could be popular and mutually advantageous: the candidate will have commenced rite of passage as early as he or she might wish (that is the moment he or she is fourteen); whilst the final element might take place at the age of sixteen or seventeen.

Hopefully, everyone gains: the candidate is enrolled and engaged upon rite of passage early; whilst the beneficiaries of mission-challenge will receive candidates who will be, in most cases, much more mature *physically* than a fourteen year old. To the extent that mission-challenge roles may incur physicality, candidates will be even more useful at sixteen or seventeen than at fourteen.

Mission-challenge has already been defined as community service. But there are onc or two questions to be asked? Should a candidate serve the community locally? Or at a location far, far away?

And playing the Devil's Advocate, there are further questions to be asked. Couldn't this five month period be better spent? Why not forget about 'mission-challenge'? It's a lofty ideal, difficult to define. Why not use the time, twenty weeks, (it could be more if necessary), serving out an apprenticeship? After all, what use is untutored youth to the community? He or she can 'hew wood and draw water' perhaps, but possibly not much more. Wouldn't young people be of better off honing their skills and looking after themselves?

Many might answer 'yes' to these questions. And the issue may one day have to be decided. At the moment it is purely academic.

For me, the answer to these questions is 'no'. If there is to be competition between rite of passage and apprenticeship, primacy lies with rite of passage. This is the time to gain experience of life. If rite of passage and apprenticeship can somehow be run in tandem, then fine. But one would want to look very closely. One doesn't want to see a candidate bogged down in minutiae or barricaded indoors swotting for an exam. Not during rite of passage.

IS AWAY, 'AWAY', ANYMORE?

Mission-challenge is a time to send candidates as far away from home as possible. As Page has shown, ritual absence is the key to success in status transformation. The human mind allows itself to believe that mystical powers are at work, and indeed they are. But it is vital to understand that there is a two-way process at work: the folk back home are 'players' too. They need their space away from candidates just as much as candidates space away from them.

The reader might be reminded of Page's explanation of the honeymoon:

> In reality, of course, the main reason many couples go away is because they feel it is expected of them: and it is expected of them because relatives and friends need a breathing space mentally to readjust to the idea that they are now husband and wife, which the wedding ceremony itself is too abrupt to provide (op. cit. p. 67)

In days of old, distance apart implied difficulty, impossibility even, of inter-communication. In today's global village, with the advent of the mobile phone and the internet, this is no longer the case. Rendering candidates incommunicado might be almost impossible to achieve. For rite of passage, this is a disaster.

We can only hope that absence from the home base, if possible at some considerable distance, will coincide with many young people's apparent desire to be free of parental and family interference. This is not true, though, for all young people. Many might not be able to assuage feelings of home-sickness.

Theoretically desirable as it might be, it would be virtually impossible to police a ban on phones and computers.

MISSION-CHALLENGE

Mission-challenge is both a mission and a challenge to the candidate. The mission is to be sent to a posting and the challenge is for the candidate to work to the best of his or her ability. The candidate will act in the role of auxiliary or volunteer. The candidate should be under supervision by rite-of-passage personnel though the degree of supervision would be bound to vary.

A candidate might be attached to an elderly person; he or she might be sent to a foreign school or be posted to a development project or be asked to work on a farm to assist with daily chores. Mission-challenge is bound to be new to a candidate's previous experience.

A further challenge to the candidate may be to operate away from home. 'Away from home' may be within his or her own culture. In such a case, the change might be not too traumatic or not traumatic at all. But 'away from home' might be abroad. In this event, culture-change might be very traumatic. The candidate would be expected to try to cope.

The key to mission-challenge will be to find candidates postings which they, the candidates, will find interesting and worthwhile. This should not be impossible. In view of the proposed length of mission-challenge it would be reasonable to enquire of a candidate's preference. It would also be reasonable to take into account what is known of a candidate's personality.

The skills period of rite of passage is conceived as obligatory for each candidate. Life-experiences are a matter of chance. But in mission-challenge, an attempt might be made to marry a candidate to the likely task ahead. A candidate's known personality, his or her personal attributes, physical disposition and personal skills (such as a foreign language) and/or gifts (musical or sports ability), likes (being outdoors) and dislikes (being outdoors!) – these can all be taken into consideration.

MISSION-CHALLENGE AND CHARITIES

Many charities offer exciting programmes. Voluntary Service Overseas (VSO), for example, currently offers a Youth for Development (YID) global education project. Its World Youth Programme 'gives young people the chance to make a real difference to community projects in the UK and overseas. Participants get the unique opportunity to live and work with another young person from a developing country for six months – spending three months in the UK and three months overseas.' The programme is currently for 17–25 year olds.

Hopefully, an organisation of VSO's experience could devise a programme for rite-of-passage candidates who are a little younger. The same might be so for other charities. One hopes that the number of charities wishing to procure the services of rite-of-passage candidates would be very considerable. The area of interest of charities is as large as life itself. The potential for mission-challenge candidates is thus enormous.

INTERNATIONAL RITE OF PASSAGE

Rite of passage may develop to be a truly international institution. Candidates who share the same language could be exchanged between countries; though they will not necessarily share the same culture. Experiencing a different culture, however, is no bad thing. Insofar as rite of passage is designed to broaden a candidate's horizons, cultural exchange is very desirable. It is also very desirable from the theoretical point of view. This has been alluded to extensively in the paragraphs above.

With all this in mind then, rite of passage for adolescents in the UK could be conducted in Australia, New Zealand or Canada; and rite of passage for children in Australia, New Zealand or Canada could be conducted in the UK. But the language of English is even more prevalent: India, the United States, Scandinavian countries – all could interchange their rite-of-passage candidates. African societies have not been included deliberately. It is exceedingly unlikely they would be prepared to sacrifice their traditional and very effective rites of passage in favour of a newly developed and initially theoretical Western alternative. It is also the case, obviously, that African customs of circumcision, infibulation and scarification are anathema to Western norms.

Whether all this would promote mutual cultural appreciation is a moot point. One hopes that it would. But the objective of rite of passage is not primarily to do this. The objective is to mature the young: to make men out of boys and women out of girls. All other beneficial outcomes are a bonus.

RITE-OF-PASSAGE MEDIA

Rite of passage could well develop its own media: newspapers, radio and television even, and that *sine qua non* of up-to-date living these days, its own blog. Candidates could and should report their rite-of-passage experiences.

A free press within rite of passage could retail good and bad news. Candidates might be also encouraged to keep a diary. Rite of passage would thus have within it the wherewithal for self-appraisal, self-improvement and reform.

Rite-of-passage media should not baulk at reporting accidents, injury and lucky escapes. The intervention of caprice and destiny in the daily lives of rite-of-passage candidates would be important news.

Introducing Chapter 36

This chapter has attempted to indicate the possible breadth of rite of passage. One baulks at involving the reader in too much needless speculation. However, before the reader can assess the overall viability of rite of passage, some idea of the possible administrative infra-structure might be given – in terms of institution and personnel.

This is the objective of the next and final chapter.

36
Suggestion For a Present-Day Rite of Passage

Administrative, Infrastructure and Personnel Roles

A new department of government

The reader is reminded that we hold that for rite of passage to be successful three basic conditions must obtain: first, the word 'rite' in rite of passage must be given life; second, rite of passage must be able to grant 'passage' – which has been held to mean 'formal transformation of personal status'; and thirdly, rite of passage must apply to all children – the catchphrase for this has been, from prince to pauper.

With this last in mind, surely nothing less than a new department of government would be necessary to administer a national programme of such a large scale. This would most likely apply to *all* viable programmes of rite of passage and certainly to this suggestion for a programme for the present-day

Many countries already have an up-and-running Ministry of Youth – France, Malaysia (youth and sport); New Zealand (youth development). Others maintain a Department for youth within a major ministry – the United Kingdom retains a Minister of State for Children within its Home Office.

The new department envisaged here might be called 'The Department of Youth Socialisation'. There's no question that the word 'socialisation' is ungainly and inelegant. But because this is new, the job should be in the name. The department's role is assuredly to promote and accomplish the *socialisation* of young people into adults. The department's title should make this clear. Socialisation is its primary objective: not education, not sport (though sport might be involved) but a total concentration on the task of assisting young people to translate from one status to another.

NEW DEPARTMENT'S ROLES

To administer the rite-of-passage programme proposed here, a new department might cover the following responsibilities:

1) To serve as a registry for *social* children, as previously defined (Chapter 31), throughout their entire period in this status (i.e. until they either graduate to early adult status having completed rite of passage or until adult status is automatically granted at 35).

2) To generate life-skill courses and life-experience events and vet agencies already in existence who might be sub-contracted to deliver them.

3) To target a programme of mission-challenge to each rite-of-passage candidate's preference and perceived abilities. To vet agencies delivering the programme. Again, many agencies may already be in existence.

4) To identify rite-of-passage staff roles and to recruit, as needed, the professional and non-professional personnel to fill them both at base and in the field.

A new department would create its own momentum. Many more responsibilities and roles would generate themselves over time.

1 SERVING AS REGISTRY

This new department will be to youth as, in the United Kingdom, the Drivers and Vehicle Licensing Authority (DVLA) is to road vehicles. Registration backed up by computer technology allows for very detailed records. The social status of every young person should be similarly recorded. One assumes that other countries will have their 'DVLA'.

Formally registering and recording children into their social status is very important.. Firstly it would insure against a young person trying to 'pass him- or her-self off' as an adult. Secondly, registration enables society, in the person of a parent, a teacher, a policeman or a judge, to say to a (social) child: 'Look! There's no point in "acting-up". We all know you're *still* a social child. Who are you trying to fool? If you want to impress, grow up properly in the prescribed way! You know what you've got to do. Get on and do it.'

'Angry young man' syndrome

The situation is however a little complicated. We cannot assume that rite-of-passage candidates will be free of wilful behaviour. Indeed, quite the opposite. It is to be expected that they may well be possessed of 'angry young man syndrome'. This was discussed earlier in Chapter 15. What was labelled there 'appallingly bad behaviour', occurs, it was shown, in highly ritualised, as well as Western, societies.

The reader is reminded of the percipient explanation of van Gennep (the author of *Les Rites de Passages*) for such juvenile delinquency. He realised that in the traditional rite-of-passage process, candidates, or 'novices' as he calls them, had to go *outside* society before they could come back into it:

> The novices are outside society, and society has no power over them, especially since they are sacred and holy, and therefore untouchable and dangerous, just as gods would be. Thus...the society is defenceless against the novices' undertakings. That is the explanation – the simplest in the world – for a fact [young people stealing and pillaging whilst awaiting initiation] that has been noted among a great many peoples and that has remained incomprehensible to observers. (van Gennep 1977. p. 114)

For a relatively short period, therefore, youngsters in highly ritualised societies are, or were, outlaws. In our own society, it seems to me, our magistrates and judiciary have been instinctively indulgent in dealing with first- and second-time young offenders. It is as if they sensed that juvenile behaviour was determined by a force, or forces, beyond juvenile control. Such a perception is spot-on. Western delinquents may not be regarded, or regard themselves, as sacred or holy; they can certainly, though, be extremely dangerous – especially if interrupted in the moment of committing an act of anti-social behaviour. This seems sometimes to release a pent-up fury. It is as if the young person has been denied an opportunity to commune with his, and nowadays again her, deepest being.

What is one to conclude from this?

Firstly, candidates may well exhibit 'angry young man' syndrome during rite of passage. We should plan for it and be happy and relieved if it does not happen.

Secondly, copying the attitude taken in traditional societies, whilst we cannot formally regard candidates as outlaws, it might be necessary, and advisable, to grant special indulgence towards candidates who behave anti-socially. This would be only for the relatively short time (a year) of rite of passage. Hopefully, a candidate's anti-social behaviour would be substantially, if not completely, modified by the restraining role of mentors. This is defined further on.

Finally, no such indulgence need be offered to social children who, for whatever reason, have decided not to embark on rite of passage. They have made their choice with its consequences.

2 GENERATING LIFE-SKILL COURSES AND LIFE-EXPERIENCE EVENTS

1 VETTING

My suggestion for a rite of passage is designed to utilise to the utmost extent the skill and expertise of existing agencies and organisations in every field we are interested in. Only in rare circumstances should it ever be necessary to create an enterprise anew. In selecting life-skill and life-experience providers, the new department should be spoilt for choice.

But all rite-of-passage courses should be vetted. The public would wish to be assured and continuously reassured that rite of passage will not become a covert centre for terrorism and subversion. A government department should always be checking to see that this never becomes so. Course providers would independently be subject to the rigour of their own professional bodies and other existing agencies such as Health and Safety.

2 GENERATING LIFE-SKILL COURSES

Generating life-skill courses should not be a problem. At the level of the first life- skill, hygiene, one would imagine that every housewife, and many a house-husband, could teach candidates how to use a washing machine, how to iron, wash, sew and mend. All one is looking for looking for is charm and charisma in the teacher.

The same applies to the suggested second life-skill, cooking. This may be a bit more technical; but there is only so much that can be taught in a week or two.

Anything more than the basics would be a plus.

The teaching of first-aid is the speciality of the Red Cross, whose credentials are too well known to be questioned. Other agencies also may impart this skill.

The fifth life-skill of map-reading (orienteering) and hiking is offered by numerous outward-bound organisations. A number of such organisations are listed in a report by the late Lord Hunt : *In Search of Adventure – a Study of Opportunities for Adventure and Challenge for Young People (1989).* Unfortunately, this excellent publication does not seem to have been updated. Many of the organisations listed in this work, if they are still extant, could provide not only this particular life-skill, but also many of the life-experiences set out in Chapter 34 – particularly those to do with dangerous sports on land, sea and in the air.

GENERATING LIFE-EXPERIENCES AND MISSION-CHALLENGE EVENTS

As for life-skills, so for life experiences. The operative principle would be for all sections of society to open themselves up for young people to encounter, witness and, wherever possible, sample what they do. Almost everybody will have some sort of role to play: 'tinker, tailor, soldier, sailor'. Perhaps the tinker, if such an occupation still exists, has little to offer – but he is part of the rhyme and makes the point that it takes the whole village, i.e. everyone in society, to raise a child. Everyone should therefore offer and devote time and play their part if called upon to do so.

As suggested, chance, based on random computer generation, should decree where candidates end up for life-experience; apart, that is, from the three proposed compulsory experiences: an encounter with dying and death; working with animals and visiting the seat/s of government.

A new department would also be able to use its government status to liaise with appropriate foreign departments and agencies. It could facilitate international rite of passage – the posting of candidates abroad on a possibly reciprocal basis, particularly during the extended and final period of rite of passage we have called mission-challenge. It could be that the whole programme of rite of passage is conducted abroad.

PERSONNEL ROLES

It would be possible to write reams about personnel required to administer the rite of passage and which roles might be filled. It would all be intensely speculative. There are two points that might be made about personnel: one general, one specific.

In general terms, if rite of passage really works, as I deeply believe it will, those dealing with juvenile delinquency will have progressively less to do. There may therefore be an opportunity to rejoice, re-train and redeploy. There should be remunerative and more positive livings in rite of passage. As stated, rite of passage will surely develop its own career structure and offer many new positions.

This leads to a statement about the cost of rite of passage. I have no doubt that rite of passage would be worth its weight in gold for the positive contribution it will make to young people's lives, so often blighted by a force that overwhelms them. The reader is reminded of the last sentence of item 9 of Chapter 1 ('The Argument'): 'anti-social behaviour is an unhealthy reaction to a natural drive'.

But I also believe that the vast financial cost of dealing with juvenile delinquency will be mitigated by the implementation of rite of passage. The positive cost of rite of passage cannot be greater than the negative cost of dealing with juvenile delinquency. Rite of passage is cheaper for society than crime of passage.

The greatest cost would be in the interstitial period whilst juvenile delinquency had yet to abate and rite of passage was inaugurated but had yet to work its magic.

A ROLE FOR MENTORS

In some traditional societies, rite-of-passage candidates are chaperoned by mentors. Candidates, male candidates particularly, are escorted. This is the way in which 'angry-young-man' syndrome, mentioned at the beginning of this chapter, is dealt with. This phenomenon is present also in traditional societies, and in Chapter 15 we presented La Fontaine's description of *litima* among the *Gisu* people of Uganda. Such was the rage of candidates that they had to be protected from themselves, and many in the community had to be protected from them. There may well be occasions when candidates in present-day rite of passage become equivalently angry and possibly nervous – two sides of the same coin.

In that traditional society mentors are recent 'graduates' who have been through the experience and know what it's all about. I would propose the mentor role for suitable and recent graduates of a present-day Western rite of passage too. Finding the first mentors might not be all that easy. But it should not be impossible.

Mentors should also be a bulwark for candidates against unwanted and predatory sexual attention. We have strongly recommended that rite of passage be delivered to each sex separately. One cannot ordain however that all encounters in rite of passage will be by members of the same sex, or indeed that that will preclude sexual interaction. One hopes that both male and female candidates will be able to 'look after themselves' by the age of fourteen, and increasingly so as the teens advance. The presence of mentors, close to the age of the candidates, and never too far away, should act as added insurance.

RITE OF PASSAGE – WHAT TO DO NOW?

We are reaching the end of what can, at this stage, be usefully said about rite of passage.

What is the next stage?

The first thing is that the basic theory be tested. This might be done for the government by academics. It could also be done by every reader reading this book.

Ask teenagers you know or come across if they believe that adulthood comes *automatically* by just *waiting* till they reach a certain age? If so, what age? And why?

The question is neutral and fairly anodyne.

A further test, less neutral and less anodyne, would be casually to begin a sentence with any young teenage, or possibly even pre-teenage, 'I'm **adol'** anai?' ('I'm **adult** aren't I?') you may come across, with the words: 'Of course, as a *child* you...'

The reaction to just this may make the case for formal rite of passage.

APPENDIX 1

QUESTIONNAIRE

1995 QUESTIONNAIRE GIVEN TO 634 YOUNG PEOPLE AGED 13–21

Thank you for taking part in this survey of young people's views. There are no right or wrong answers to these questions – just your opinion.

1. Do you regard yourself as an adult?	No / Yes
2. If you have replied 'No', at approximately what age *will* you become adult?	Age of ......
3. If you have replied 'Yes', at approximately what age *did* you become adult?	Age of ......
4. Do you think your friends regard you as adult?	Yes / No
5. Do you regard your friends as adult?	No / Yes
6. Do you think adulthood comes automatically by just waiting till you reach a certain age?	Yes / No
7. If you have replied 'Yes', what is this age?	Age of ......
8. At the age that you are now, do you expect people to recognise your maturity?	Do not expect / Do expect
9. Is it important to you that people, especially people your own age, should know from the way you conduct yourself that you expect to be treated as an adult?	Important / Not Important
10. Males and females, socially speaking, mature into adults in different ways and by different processes?	Disagree / Agree
11. Full adult status has to be earned?	Agree / Disagree
Finally, how old are you at the moment?	.... years .... months

RESULTS IN PERCENTAGES

Proposition	School				All		Young Offenders (104)	
	Yes	*No*	*Yes*	*No*	*Yes*	*No*	*Yes*	*No*
1. Do you regard yourself as an adult?	43	57	43	57	43	57	80	20
2. If you have replied 'No', at approximately what age *will* you become adult?	*Results to these questions were incomplete and inconclusive*							
3. If you have replied 'Yes', at approximately what age *did* you become adult?								
4. Do you think your friends regard you as adult?	40	60	42	58	41	59	81	19
5. Do you regard your friends as adult?	40	60	46	54	42	58	82	18
6. Do you think adult-hood comes automatically by just waiting till you reach a certain age?	20	80	14	86	18	82	23	77
7. If you have replied 'Yes', what is this age?	*Results to these questions were incomplete and inconclusive*							
8. At the age that you are now, do you expect people to recognise your maturity?	84	16	91	9	86	14	72	28
9. Is it important to you that people, especially people your own age, should know from the way you conduct your-self that you expect to be treated as an adult?	68	32	67	33	68	32	64	36
10. Males and females, socially speaking, mature into adults in different ways and by different processes?	83	17	92	8	86	14	87	13
11. Full adult status has to be earned?	65	35	65	35	65	35	62	38

BREAKDOWN OF RESPONDENTS

Participants		**No. of Institutions**	**Respondents**
Secondary Schools	Mixed Sex, State, Secular	3	143
	Mixed Sex, State, Religious	1	102
	Single Sex, State, Boys	1	84
	Single Sex, State, Girls	1	51
Private, fee-paying, non-boarding, boys		1	116
College of Further Education		3	34
Young Offender Institutions		3	104
Totals		***13***	***634***

	Ages	**13–14**	**14–15**	**15–16**	**16–17**	**17–18**	**18–19**	**19–20**	**21**	*Totals*
Schoolchildren	**boys**	19	123	73	57	57	6	0	0	***335***
	girls	15	74	64	22	17	3	0	0	***195***
Young offenders		0	4	7	16	23	22	26	6	***104***
Totals		***34***	***201***	***144***	***95***	***97***	***31***	***26***	***6***	***634***

INTERPRETATION AND COMMENT

Two responses in particular reinforce principles independently derived from the observation of highly ritualised societies: one, is the answer given by both sexes to question 10; the other, the responses given to questions 6 and 11.

Question 10 suggested that males and females, socially speaking, mature into adults in different ways and by a different process. Females (92 vs 8) are even more emphatic than males (83 vs 17) in agreeing with this proposition. One is surely entitled to conclude from this that delivering a rite-of-passage programme on an individual sex basis is wholly correct. This replicates the position in most highly ritualised societies.

Proposition 6 asks respondents whether they think adulthood comes automatically by just waiting till you reach a certain age. Only 18% concurred with this proposition; 82% did not. It is not unreasonable to conclude from this that the vast majority of young people feel they have to do something for adulthood to come. The only question is: what?

Proposition 11 reinforces proposition six by suggesting full adult status has to be earned. Almost uniformly, two thirds of respondents agreed with this proposition. Taken together with the results of proposition 6 above, one is again entitled to conclude that a lot of youth crime and adolescent anti-social behaviour can legitimately be regarded as the 'adult status earning' process in action.

The responses to proposition 8 (at the age you are now, do you expect people to recognise your maturity? Yes, 86%; No, 14%) tells us that the acquisition of respect and adult status is an overriding aspiration for young people. Perhaps, noting this, the responses given to questions 1, 4 and 5 may be seen as slightly self-deprecatory.

Finally, readers may be interested to learn that a very small survey of the same questions was conducted in September 2008 among just 92 children at a fee-paying, mixed-sex secondary school. A comparison of the results, in percentages, is as follows:

	Boys and Girls			
	1995 (*530)		**2008 (92)**	
	Yes (%)	**No (%)**	**Yes (%)**	**No (%)**
1. Do you regard yourself as adult?	43	57	27	73
4. Do you think your friends regard you as adult?	41	59	21	79
5. Do you regard your friends as adult?	42	58	18	82
6. Do you think adult comes automatically...?	18	82	22	78
8. At the age that you are now, do you expect people...?	86	14	85	15
9. It's important to you, that especially people your own age...?	68	32	53	47
10. Males and females, socially speaking, mature into adults...?	86	14	87	13
11. Full adult status has to be earned?	65	35	65	35

**Total figure for Boys and Girls minus the 104 Young Offenders.*

Conclusion: In thirteen years (1995–2008), nothing much has changed!

APPENDIX 2

CRIME IN JAPAN

Fenwick (2000) has reproduced crime statistics for post-war Japan, taking his figures from various sources. One source, Fukuyama (1999) compares Japan with England and Wales, Sweden and the United States; others, such as van Dijk and Mayhew (1992), offer a wider scope – including more European countries as well as Canada, New Zealand and Australia.

Fukuyama's figures cover the period 1950–96 in two year segments. His figures for 'Total Violent Crime' show Japan starting in 1950 above England and Wales, and the United States, at 140 per 100,000 of the population. England and Wales were 40 per 100,000 of the population, and the United States just over 100. But by 1996, Japan had declined from 140 to just 40; England and Wales, on the other hand had shot up to nearly 700, and the United States to just over 600 violent crimes per 100,000 of the population.

Fukuyama's figures for 'Theft' show a similar pattern. Once again, Japan in 1950 produced approximately 1,200 theft crimes per 100,000 of the population, very slightly above England & Wales (1,000), but below the United States (1,800). The Japanese graph line remains absolutely static from 1950 to 1996, staying at 1,200 theft crimes per 100,000 of the population. By 1996, England and Wales and the United States had increased to 6,000 and 4,200 respectively.

Van Dijk and Mayhew (1992) measure 'Assault Rates' in terms of assault crimes per 1,000 of the population. For the year 1991, their chart shows Japan at zero, yes zero, crimes per 1,000. Italy and Belgium centre around 0.5; Sweden, Czechoslovakia, England and Wales at 1.5; Poland, Netherlands, Finland and the United States at just under 2; Canada, New Zealand and Australia at just under 2.5.

Japan (1 per 100,000 of the population) demonstrated for the year 1998 homicide figures three times less than the United Kingdom (3 per 100,000) and nine times less of the United States (9 per 100,000).

Japan's population (127.4 million) is more than double the United Kingdom's (60.7 million). Her land area of 146,000 sq. miles is 65% greater than the United Kingdom's (88,745). Much of this increase in size is obviated by mountainous terrain. Thus Japan's crime figures are reproduced in areas of high concentration of urban population.

To what extent these crimes of violence, theft and assault in different countries have been compared like for like is difficult to tell. Suffice to say, however, that the sources cited are professional in their field. Furthermore, juvenile crime is subsumed within these figures. There is no reason to believe that Japan reproduces figures for juvenile crime proportionately different from crime as a whole. In other words, juvenile crime in Japan is low – a reflection of the overall crime figures. There may or may not have been recent changes, but for the latter half of the twentieth century, Japan has remained stable, whilst figures in Western society have shot up.

We have claimed that tight regulation of personal status underpins Japanese stability. If this is the case, it is borne out by Japanese crime figures which do great credit to this highly ritualised society from which we have so much to learn.

BIBLIOGRAPHY

Barbour, I.G. 1974. *Myths, Models and Paradigms: A Comparative Study in Science and Religion*. New York: Harper & Row.

Blumenkrantz, D. 1966 *The Rite Way: Guiding Youth to Adulthood and the Problem of Communitas*. UMI Dissertation Services, Ann Arbor, Michigan.

Brain, R. 1979. *Rites, Black and White*. Victoria: Penguin Books, Australia

Burt, C. 1938. *The Young Delinquent*. (Third and revised edition.) London: University of London Press.

Chapman, A.H. 1968. *Put-offs and Come-ons: Psychological Manoeuvres and Stratagems*. London: Transworld Publishers.

Concise Oxford Dictionary. 1998 (Ninth edition.) New York: Oxford University Press.

Durkheim, E. 1982. *The Rules of Sociological Method and Selected Texts on Sociology and its Method*. Edited with an introduction by Steven Lukes. London: MacMillan Education.

Eliade, M. 1960. *Myths, Dreams and Mysteries*. New York: Harper & Row.

Eliade, M. 1963. *Myth and Reality*. New York: Harper & Row.

Fenwick C.R. 2000. 'Education, Neighbourhood, and the Police: Interpreting Serious Street Crime Patterns in Postwar Japan (1950-2000)'. A Paper for St. Anthony's Jubilee Conference, Oxford University, July 2000.

Fukuyama, F. 1999. *The Great Disruption: Human Nature and the Reconstitution of Social Order*. New York: The Free Press.

Gluckman, M. 1966. *Custom and Conflict in Africa*. Oxford: Basil Blackwell.

Hendry, J. 1987. *Understanding Japanese Society*. Beckenham, Kent: Croom Helm.

Hendry, J 1993. *Wrapping Culture: Politeness, Presentation, and Power in Japan and other Societies*. Oxford: Oxford University Press.

Home Office 1991. Cm 2134 *Criminal Statistics England and Wales*. London: Her Majesty's Stationery Office.

Home Office 2008. *Home Office Statistical Bulletin. Crime in England and Wales 2006/2007*. (Eds: S. Nicholas, C. Kershaw and A. Walker.) London: Her Majesty's Stationery Office.

House of Commons Factsheet No. 52. April 2000. *Some Traditions and Customs of The House of Commons*. London: House of Commons Public Information Office.

Hunt, J. (ed.) 1989. *In Search of Adventure: A Study of Opportunities for Adventure and Challenge for Young People*. Guildford, Surrey: Talbot Adair Press.

Knight, S 1983. *The Brotherhood, the Secret World of the Freemasons*. London: Panther Books, Granada Publishing.

Kuhn, T. 1970. *The Structure of Scientific Revolutions*. Chicago, Illinois: University of Chicago Press.

La Fontaine, J. 1985. *Initiation: Ritual Drama and Secret Knowledge Across the World*. Harmondsworth, Middlesex: Penguin Books.

Levine, D.K. 1965. *Wax and Gold*. University of Chicago Press.
Marsh, P., Rosser, E. and Harré, R. 1987 (first published 1978). *The Rules of Disorder.* London: Routledge & Kegan Paul.
Page, M. 1972. *The Company Savage: Life in the Corporate Jungle.* London: Cassell.
Robbins, A. 2003. *Secrets of the Tomb, Skull and Bones, The Ivy League, and the Hidden Paths of Power.* Boston, Mass.: Little, Brown and Company.
Roose-Evans, J. 1994. *Passages of the Soul: Ritual Today.* Dorset, United Kingdom: Element Books Ltd.
Russell, B. 1945. *History of Western Philosophy.* London: George Allen & Unwin.
Russell, B. 1956. *Portraits from Memory and Other Essays.* London: George Allen & Unwin.
Saitoti, Tepilit Ole. 1988 (first published 1980). *Maasai.* London: Elm Tree Books.
Sharpe, K. 1984. *From Science to an Adequate Mythology.* Auckland, New Zealand: Interface Press.
Shirer, W.L. 1971 (eighth printing). *The Rise and Fall of the Third Reich.* London: Pan Books.
Somé, M. 1993. *Ritual: Power, Healing and Community.* Portland, Oregon: Swan Raven.
Somé, M. 1994. *Of Water and the Spirit: Ritual, Magic and Initiation in the Life of an African Shaman.* New York: Putnam & Sons.
Szasz, T. 1973. *The Second Sin.* New York: Doubleday.
Takao, S. 1978. *Japanese and the Japanese: Words in Culture.* Tokyo: Kodansha International Ltd.
van Dijk, J.J.M. and Mayhew, P. 1992. *Criminal Victimisation in the Industrialised World : Key Findings of the 1989 and 1992 International Crime Surveys.* The Hague: Ministry of Justice.
van Gennep, A. 1977. *The Rites of Passage.* (Translated by Monika B. Vizedom and Gabrielle L. Caffee. Introduction to the English edition by Solon T. Kimball.) London: Routledge and Kegan Paul.
Whyte, W., Greenwood, D. and Lazes, P. 1991. "Participatory Action Research: Through Practice to Science in Social Research." In Whyte, W,. (ed.), *Participatory Action Research.* Newbury Park, California, US: Sage Publications Inc.
Yokohama M. 1999. 'Trends of Organized Crime by Borykudan in Japan', *Organized Crime: Uncertainties and Dilemmas.* Chicago: Office of International Criminal Justice.

INDEX

Printed in the United Kingdom
by Lightning Source UK Ltd.
133916UK00001B/79-522/P

9 789650 902667